Augustus Toplady

AUGUSTUS TOPLADY

Douglas Bond

PUBLISHING WITH A MISSION

EP BOOKS
Faverdale North
Darlington
DL3 0PH, England

web: http://www.epbooks.org

e-mail: sales@epbooks.org

First published 2012

British Library Cataloguing in Publication Data available

ISBN 13: 978-0-85234-793-5   ISBN-10: 0-85234-793-6

Printed and bound in Great Britain by the MPG Books Group,
Bodmin and King's Lynn.

To my wife

Contents

INTRODUCTION

What are we to make of a man described as 'strangely compounded, peculiarly constituted, and oddly framed'? It conjures up in the mind an image of Stevenson's Mr Hyde, or Shelley's Frankenstein, or Hugo's Quasimodo. But that is how J. C. Ryle (1816–1900) describes Augustus Montague Toplady (1740–1778), author of what has been called the best-loved English hymn. One wonders why someone would bother writing a biography — or reading one — about a strange, peculiar, odd person. Nevertheless, Ryle declared that no account of Christianity in England in the eighteenth century would be complete without featuring remarkable Toplady. In Ryle's words:

> Not one of his contemporaries surpassed him, and hardly any equalled him. He was a man of rare grace and gifts, and one who left his mark very deeply on his own generation. For soundness in the faith, singleness of eye, and devotedness of life, he deserves to be ranked with Whitefield, or Grimshaw, or Romaine.

This is exalted company with which Ryle ranks Toplady. Moreover, consider that Toplady had many fewer years in which to achieve worthiness of that ranking: George Whitefield (1714–1770) outlived Toplady by nearly twenty years, William Grimshaw (1708–1763) by about the same, and William Romaine (1714–1795) lived over forty years longer — more than twice Toplady's lifetime. Yet Ryle ranks Toplady on a level with these giants, all of whom lived decades longer than he. It is nothing short of remarkable that in his brief life Toplady achieved the foremost rank as scholar, theologian, pastor, and hymn-writer.

Not everyone, however, has shared Ryle's exalted opinion of Toplady. His was a life of sometimes bitter contending for gospel orthodoxy in the Age of Reason. And for this contending he was dismissed by critics as 'a wild beast of impatience and lion-like fury', an extreme Calvinist, a copper-bottomed controversialist, and a 'chimney sweeper'.

But today we are far more likely to be simply ignorant of Toplady. People who know something about eighteenth-century Christianity, who might actually recognize his name, may connect his name with a hymn; but more likely he will be remembered as the vitriolic controversialist with John Wesley. Politely pushed to the side; end of story. I find that the more I think I know about someone, about whom I actually know very little, the more certain it is that I will draw distorted conclusions about that person.

The story of Toplady's life is a prime example of my tendency to draw ultimate conclusions about someone based on very partial information. I am apparently not alone in this. 'There is hardly any man of [Toplady's] calibre', laments Ryle, 'of whom so little is known. [He was, however,] most loved where he was most known.' He further laments that those who bother to learn about Toplady primarily remember his frailties.

Two years before Toplady was born, on 24 May 1738, John Wesley (1703–1791), newly returned from the American colonies, found himself in a building only a few yards from where the London Museum stands today. He gave this account of what transpired:

> In the evening I went very unwillingly to a society in Aldersgate Street, where one was reading Luther's preface to the Epistle to the Romans. About a quarter before nine, while he was describing the change which God works in the heart through faith in Christ, I felt my heart strangely warmed. I felt I did trust in Christ alone for salvation; and an assurance was given me that He had taken away my sins, even mine, and saved me from the law of sin and death.

Alas, in later years Wesley and Toplady would square off and plant their flags in one of church history's bitterest battles over the meaning of the gospel and of grace. One wonders if the two would have become such intractable enemies had Wesley continued expressing his conversion in terms of 'the change which God works in the heart' and declaring that he 'did trust in Christ alone for salvation.' In any event, it would be Toplady's wrangling with Wesley about salvation that would most expose his frailties and yet also his remarkable gifts and graces.

Toplady and grace

'He was a man in whom there was a most extraordinary mixture of grace and infirmity', wrote Ryle. 'Hundreds, unhappily, know much of his infirmities who know little of his graces.'

Grace was a constant theme for Toplady: in his hymns, in his theological works, and in his private entries in his diary. He never wearied of or grew bored with God's free grace in the gospel. Nothing could divert him from speaking and writing about it. In an entry dated 31 December 1767, he wrote, 'Upon a review of the past year, I desire to confess that my unfaithfulness has been exceeding great; my sins still greater; God's mercies greater than both.' Reflecting on this stage in his short life, he concluded: 'My shortcomings and my misdoings, my unbelief and want of love, would sink me into the lowest hell, was not Jesus my righteousness and my Redeemer.'

Heartfelt reflections on his unworthiness and Christ's immeasurable worth appear everywhere in Toplady's diary and devotional writings. But it would be in Toplady's hymns that he would immortalize for the ages his intimate knowledge of and dependence on the free grace of God in Jesus, his righteousness and Redeemer. It was the Archbishop of the Church of Ireland, and husband of Irish hymn-writer Cecil Frances Alexander, who said after his wife's death in 1895, 'The theologian is for the educated few; the preacher is for one generation; the hymn-writer speaks an imperishable language.'

The Archbishop goes on to say that the poet who writes hymns 'bequeaths to all the ages the music of immortal words.' Though he is remembered today primarily for one hymn — and that one a perennial favourite — it was in one of Toplady's lesser-known hymns that he so memorably placards for us the centrality of the grace of God:

Grace, 'tis a charming sound,
Harmonious to the ear;
Heaven with the echo shall resound,
And all the earth shall hear.

Each quatrain thereafter begins with the word 'Grace' and
explores, with poetic skill and simplicity, the beautiful
intricacies of the gospel of grace. Toplady understood grace
so well because he understood the sinfulness of his own
heart so thoroughly, as he so often expressed it in his diary
and other writings. After a Lord's Day of particularly fruitful
ministry, 2 October 1768, he wrote these words: 'How is it,
O thou God of love, that thy tender mercies should thus
accompany and follow the vilest sinner out of hell! That,
to me, who am less than the least of all saints, this grace
should be given, that I should both experience and preach
the unsearchable riches of Christ!' So consistent is this man's
sense of his own unworthiness in his writings, that we have
every reason to believe that this was no self-deprecating
pretence; he really thought this way about himself — and,
hence, about Christ and his love. Nevertheless, history has
largely ignored Toplady's keen awareness of and candid
admission of his unworthiness, preferring to feature more
his sins and dwell more lingeringly upon his infirmities
than upon the grace of Christ on which Toplady so utterly
depended.

It is, therefore, the purpose of this book to pull back the
shroud that has covered Toplady, to unmask the caricature
that has shaped his memory as merely a raw-boned and
harsh controversialist. Since his infirmities are better
known and more easily remembered, it is the purpose of this

succinct biography of Toplady to make known more widely and clearly his pastoral, theological, and poetic graces; and to do so with honesty, fairness, and candour.

Toplady's world

The eighteenth-century world into which Toplady was born was a time of great intellectual achievement: philosophers soaring into the heights of human reason; political theorists formulating treatises on government and economics; scientists discovering the intricacies of human anatomy and making significant advances in medicine; and musicians, architects, painters, and poets creating magnificent, culture-defining art.

There were luminaries aplenty in Toplady's world. Three years before Toplady's birth, Samuel Johnson (1709–1784) had left his home in Lichfield and come to London, there to write his epic poem named for the city, and later to compile his famous dictionary. Johnson's Literary Club, with which Toplady would have some associations, began meeting at the Turk's Head Inn, with more informal gatherings at various London coffee shops and public houses. James Boswell (1740–1795), Johnson's companion and justly famous biographer, was born the same year as Toplady.

Meanwhile in 1740, the year of Toplady's birth, John Wesley translated from German the hymn 'Jesus, Thy Blood and Righteousness'. And a few months later, when Toplady was cutting his first teeth, Jonathan Edwards (1703–1758) delivered his famous sermon, *Sinners in the Hands of an Angry God*, on 8 July 1741, at Second Meeting House, Enfield, Connecticut. When Toplady was eight months old, the famous violinist and composer Antonio Vivaldi (1678–1741) died in Vienna. By September of the same year, George Frederick Handel (1685–1759) had completed in a mere twenty-four days his incomparable oratorio, 'The Messiah.'

Why Toplady is for today

Toplady lived out his nearly thirty-eight short years in Enlightenment England, the so-called Age of Reason. Rationalism had made its way into the theology, worship, and preaching of the church to produce deism and a resurgent semi-Pelagianism. And although the eighteenth century also saw the Great Awakening, when the Spirit of God was moving mightily in Britain and throughout the American colonies, often what it is remembered for is a moralistic deism that denied the sovereign power of God alone to transform sinners into saints by grace alone. Unflinching, Toplady took his stand against such preachers and such preaching. Just as Paul got worked up when men distorted the gospel in his day (Galatians 1:6-9), so did Toplady.

But that is in the past. Distorting the gospel is all behind the church today, right? Sadly, it is not. Not when we have men in confessional pulpits telling their congregations that they are tired of propaganda buzz words like 'gospel' and 'grace' — Toplady would never have said this. Not when we have ministers who claim to be preaching in the historic tradition of the Reformation but who declare that 'we determine our destiny by our faith and our obedience' — nor would he preach this. Not when we have men preaching justification by faithfulness and calling Christ-centred preaching a fad — nor would he do this. Not when we have learned preachers who make sanctification a condition of justification, who declare that the elect can forfeit their salvation by unfaithfulness — Toplady would rather have been accursed than preach anything like this.

Make no mistake, the gospel is in the crosshairs of the Enemy in every generation, and that is why it is imperative that we rise up in our day and contend for the faith once delivered to the saints (Jude 1:3).

Since the church is never far from abandoning the good news for the bad news, never far from becoming suspicious of free grace and returning to a syncretistic grace-and-obedience distortion of the gospel, we need to drink deeply of the life and ministry of a man like Augustus Montague Toplady, a 'debtor to mercy alone'.

TIMELINE

1776	American colonies declared independence from Britain
1778	Died on 11 August, of tuberculosis, aged thirty-seven
1779	Newton and Cowper publish the *Olney Hymns*

1

BIRTH AND EARLY LIFE

Two months after naval Commander George Anson (1697–1762) sailed from England on his famous circumnavigation of the globe, Richard and Catherine Toplady also set out on a journey. Commissioned in the Royal Marines in 1739, Richard Toplady was likely on his way to Portsmouth and deployment to fight in Spanish Columbia in the War of Jenkin's Ear, his wife accompanying him to his ship. Forty-two miles southwest of London, however, they halted at the town of Farnham in Surrey. His wife Catherine was in labour. Since their first child, Francis, had died only days after birth, the Topladys may have been understandably anxious. Richard knew he had to find a comfortable place for his wife to give birth. There could be no delay. After making inquiries, Richard secured a cottage on West Street. There (in a house which no longer stands), on 4 November 1740, Catherine gave birth to a boy. They named him Augustus Montague Toplady.

It was November, and weather in England at such a time of the year is generally wet, windy, and cold. Nevertheless, the new parents made the short but blustery walk down the street to St. Andrew's Parish Church and had their son christened in the Church of England, his baptism recorded in the church records on 29 November 1740. St. Andrew's was built in the twelfth century on the site of a Saxon church, and is a gem of Gothic architecture, with a timbered roof and a history of fires. The present nave, the one in which Catherine and Richard Toplady would have presented their son for baptism, was built in the fifteenth century.

What happened in the first weeks and months of Toplady's life is a mystery. Richard served under the command of his friend Admiral Vernon, whose family home was in Farnham, so it is possible that they had come to the town intentionally because of their connection to the Vernons. There is no record of how long Richard remained with his young family in Farnham after Toplady's birth. But it could not have been long.

In times of war, duty calls, and, then as now, newborn sons are not regarded as an impediment to fulfilling one's military commission. Within weeks or months, Major Richard Toplady must have packed his things, kissed his wife and son goodbye, and joined his ship in Portsmouth, from there sailing for South America and war. In March 1741, at one of Spain's most important trading ports, the British launched a major amphibious attack. The Siege of Cartagena proved disastrous for England, with many casualties from combat, and still more from yellow fever. Major Richard Toplady was one of those casualties.

Back in England, Prime Minister Robert Walpole (1676–1745) was blamed for the crushing defeat, and a new government was installed. There is no surviving record of how Catherine Toplady received the news of her husband's death, and exactly what she did next. Although Catherine's father, a Rev. Richard Bate, had been an Anglican clergyman near Canterbury, she appears not to have taken her son to where she might have had relatives. What is clear is her devotion to her son and his well-being. Of his mother, Toplady always wrote in the most endearing terms, and she was described as 'a woman of piety, elegance, and taste'. She may have stayed on in Farnham, in which case Toplady would likely have begun his schooling there.

One of Toplady's boyhood diary entries gives us a warm vignette of his mother's influence and spiritual nurture in her son's life: 'My dear mamma, having heard my prayers, cried tears for joy, and said that she hoped I should never leave the right road, and bid me beware cautiously of sin, that God's heavenly grace might be with me'. Dear woman that she must have been, her understanding of the gospel may have been coloured by the rising tide of rationalism in the Church of England. If his account of her words is accurate, she seems to have been urging him to 'beware of sin' so that he might, by avoiding sin, win 'God's heavenly grace', which hardly sounds like the justification by faith alone of which Toplady would become such a passionate and devoted defender.

London and Westminster School

Catherine Toplady eventually returned to London with her son, perhaps when he was nine or ten years old. We are left to conjecture about the specific circumstances, but Toplady's mother managed to secure for her son a place at the prestigious Westminster School, known then as 'the cradle of the Muses'. The cathedral school of Westminster, positioned where it has stood in all its Gothic splendour for centuries east of the Dean's Yard and directly south of the great abbey, had since the early seventeenth century been one of the greatest preparatory schools in England. This 'School of Poetry', as it has been called, produced many notable poets and hymn-writers. Charles Wesley (1707–1788) began his studies there in 1716, and in 1742 — when Toplady was but a toddler — William Cowper (1731–1800) arrived in London to begin his studies at Westminster School.

Somewhere around 1749, Toplady found himself a student at Westminster School. Cowper left Westminster in 1749, and though there would have been nearly a ten-year difference in their ages, they may have seen each other — perhaps daily in chapel — and it is entirely possible that they may have met. Meanwhile, Charles Wesley was writing his incomparable hymn that began, 'Thou hidden source of calm repose, thou all sufficient love divine'.

On opening day, the daunting reputation of the school may have struck fear into Toplady's young imagination. He was seated in the thirteenth-century vaulted monks' dormitory, now a schoolroom that had in years past been presided over by Richard Busby (1606–1695), the infamous 'Flogging Master'. But Toplady sat gazing up at the wigged and robed figure of the present headmaster, seventy-year-old Dr John Nicholl. Though the birch switch was never far from hand, it was seldom used, and Nicholl would prove to be a gentle teacher who inspired love and respect in his students.

Under Nicholl's tutelage Westminster School would live up to its name as the 'cradle of the Muses'. Here Toplady would show considerable interest and ability in learning. He developed the habit of writing down his thoughts and prayers in a diary, praying on his way to lessons that he would 'not have any anger from Dr. Nicholl' or the other masters. And on leaving the schoolroom, he would express his gratitude for the opportunity to learn: 'Thanks be to Thee for my progress in learning, and for all Thy goodness, kindnesses, and comforts. Amen.' For his progress in learning at Westminster School there was a good deal for which to be thankful. Most notably, it was here that he learned to read and love poetry, and to begin writing poetry of his own.

Boys and depravity being what they are, when dozens of nine-year-old boys are housed in close quarters in a boarding school, feathers and fists will fly. Realizing his tendency toward entering the fray, Toplady wrote a daily prayer confessing his sins and asking God to help him overcome them. When he was eleven he took stock of his progress. 'I praise God I can remember no dreadful crime; and not to me but to the Lord be the glory, Amen.' After his conversion to Christ, Toplady's self-assessment would go to the root, to the condition of his heart; and he then concluded: 'I am less than nothing.'

Filling gaps

One of the reasons why there are so many blank places in Toplady's story, ones that must be filled in by informed conjecture, is that he was an only child, he never married, and, therefore, had no children of his own to collect all the pieces of his life's story together while the historical trail was still fresh. Hence, the historian is left to fill in the gaps in his diary and other writings with comparative historical context that sheds light on the lesser-illuminated episodes in Toplady's life.

For instance, we know from a diary entry near his twelfth year that he had a difficult aunt to contend with: 'Aunt Betsy is so vastly quarrelsome, in short, she is so fractious, and captious, and insolent, that she is unfit for human society'. My experience with twelve-year-olds is that they don't always get things perfectly accurate, and so we must be cautious of being overly hard on Aunt Betsy here. Nevertheless, there are some illuminating dimensions in this entry. What twelve-year-old do I know who has developed this breadth of vocabulary, who can string together so many multi-syllabic words to describe a less-than-favourite relative? Moreover, there may be, in these lines, hints of what would prove to be Toplady's infirmity, his own tendency to make sometimes excessive criticisms of those with whom he disagreed. Perhaps poor Aunt Betsy had more sway over her nephew than either she or young Augustus realized. We also learn that Toplady began preaching when he was twelve. Since there was no vast cyber-repository for sermons then, we have no record of what those sermons sounded like. Toplady does record in his diary that an uncle found one of his written sermons, read it, and, certain his nephew could not have written such a sermon, asked whose it was and where he had gotten it.

By his fourteenth year, Toplady had developed strong opinions about the varying merits of sermons and preachers. On Sunday 27 January 1754, Toplady gave a brief and scathing account of a sermon he had endured in London: 'Went to St. Martin's Church. Heard a poor, mean sermon, and a very long one, by Dr. Pearce, Bishop of Bangor. The only good thing in it was when he said, "To conclude"'. Not only does this glimpse reveal Toplady's wit, this episode of hearing a long and pedantic sermon at the famous St. Martin-in-the-Fields, near Trafalgar Square, and others in its category, probably helped shape Toplady's own sense of what good preaching was supposed to be.

The young poet

While trying his adolescent hand at crafting good sermons, essays, and plays, he continued writing poetry. It is not overly surprising that it was while he was at Westminster School, 'The School of Poetry', Toplady first began seriously attempting to write poetry. His early efforts were crude and halting, as was — by his own admission — his grasp of eternal truths:

> Father, Lord of all mankind,
> Thee we attempt to sing.

'Attempt' seems here to be the operative word. These lines fall considerably short of scaling Parnassus and are a rather wooden attempt at best. Though Toplady was not a naturally gifted poet — few rank his poetic endowment alongside Isaac Watts (1674–1748) or his contemporary William Cowper — nevertheless, the best of the hymns written in his spiritual maturity would greatly surpass his juvenile poetic efforts, and a select few of them would rank among the finest hymns in the language.

It is impossible to quantify what percentage of a hymn-writer's achievement is innate gift and what is the result of growth in grace, and in spiritual imagination, and in the deepest, most passionate and intimate grasp of eternal beauties. Yet, if the greatness of a man's poetry takes into account his lack of innate poetic giftedness, on the one hand, and on the other, the enduring place at least one of his hymns — 'Rock of Ages' — has achieved since his death, then Toplady must be ranked among the very finest of English hymn-writers.

But hymn-writing of merit would come later. At fourteen, Toplady got it in his head that he would write 'a farce', a play to be performed at Drury Lane. He even managed to have an audience with the famous London actor, David Garrick (1717–1779), and presented his play and asked him to perform it. Garrick humoured the teen and told him to return at the end of the season.

The rulemaker

As a boy, precocious Toplady seems to have had a propensity toward spiritual pride as he was a great rule maker for himself. In an entry while still early in his years of study at Westminster, he wrote,

> I set down these rules: First, I must beware of spiritual pride: secondly, of uncleanness: thirdly, of lying: fourthly, of neglecting that great precept of loving God with all my heart, mind and strength. The love of God consists in a thorough obedience to His mandates, which gives such pleasing ideas that the soul is transported in a manner beyond itself.

In Toplady's boyhood diary, written several years before his spiritual awakening and conversion, there is a great deal of law, but little or nothing of the grace of the gospel. There is a great deal of religious moralism here — something highly valued in Enlightenment England — but little or nothing of the passionate feeling of wonder at redeeming love (he spends more time schooling himself on loving God than reflecting on God loving him). And there is almost nothing of Christ, his atoning sacrifice and imputed righteousness — themes that would saturate everything Toplady would write after the spiritual transformation he would soon undergo in his conversion.

2

CONVERSION AND COLLEGE

'I am of Ireland', wrote poet William Butler Yeats (1865–1939), 'the Holy Land of Ireland'. Toplady was not from Ireland, but his father seems to have had Irish connections. After five or six years of study at Westminster School, Toplady and his mother appear next in Ireland, the land of poetry. The details of how he and his mother made this move are sketchy at best. In a comment to a friend he mentioned something about his father's property. So it may have been that a relative died, leaving some property to Toplady and his mother. Another suggestion is that his mother had been made heir of some property in Wexford. For whatever reason, teenage Toplady and his mother moved to Ireland, where on 11 July 1756, he began his studies at Trinity College, Dublin.

From the 'School of Poetry' at Westminster, Toplady, in the providence of God, was next at an institution of learning that would help train at least two other hymn-writers of note: Irish Thomas Kelly (1769–1855), author of the weighty passion hymn based on Isaiah 53, 'Stricken, Smitten, and Afflicted'; and the Scot, James Montgomery (1771–1854), author of the rousing hymn of worship, 'Stand Up and Bless the Lord, Ye People of His Choice'. Incidentally, Irish poet William Butler Yeats much later received an honorary degree from Trinity College, Dublin.

Conversion

Only months before Toplady began studying at Trinity College, Dublin, a great earthquake rocked the British Isles: 'The earth was disturbed by lightnings, thunders, and threats of heaven'. Fifteen-year-old Toplady, living with his mother near a place named Codymain (or Cooladine), was troubled by the event. While musing on the earthquake, he learned of a man who was preaching in a nearby barn. Though Toplady had been raised in the elite halls of High Church Anglicanism, and would have been scornful of such a gathering in such a place, nevertheless, he had heard plenty of bad preaching from Anglicans, so he was curious.

In the mysterious workings of the Spirit of God, Toplady found himself sitting in an Irish barn, listening to an uneducated Irishman by the name of James Morris preach a sermon. Teenage Toplady, highly educated and opinionated, may well have gone ready and eager to find fault. And then James Morris rose to his feet and opened his Bible to Ephesians 2:13 and read out in his Irish brogue, 'Ye who were sometimes far off are made nigh by the blood of Christ'. The zealous but untrained layman's words transfixed young Toplady. It was a sermon like none he had ever heard before. And there was no place for his critical wit in the man's words.

The powerful effect of this unlettered man's words on Toplady's heart is a potent reminder that the Holy Spirit can speak through anyone, can make beautiful the feet of anyone who brings the good tidings of the gospel of peace. Toplady marked his conversion from August 1756. Later in his diary, he reflected with gratitude on the mercy of God in his conversion:

> Strange that I, who had so long sat under the means of grace in England, should be brought nigh to God in an obscure part of Ireland, amidst a handful of God's people met together in a barn, and under the ministry of one who could hardly spell his name! Surely it was the Lord's doing, and is marvellous! The excellency of such power must be of God, and cannot be of man. The regenerating Spirit breathes not only on whom, but likewise when, where, and as he listeth.

Much of the detail of what Toplady did during the next two years is unknown, but his gratitude for the man who was God's instrument in his conversion never flagged. James Morris may have been a Methodist, though there is evidence that he later became a Baptist preacher. Either way, Toplady revered the unlettered man who had faithfully preached Christ in that Irish barn. In an entry in his diary dated 1 August 1760, Toplady described hiring a horse and a man to guide him, and setting out to visit 'my dear brother [James] Morris, that precious follower of the Lamb'. Ten years later, Toplady gave further tribute to Morris in a diary entry dated 29 February 1768:

> At night, after my return from Exeter, my desires were strongly drawn out, and drawn up to the Lord. I could indeed say that I groaned with groans of love, joy, and peace; but so

it was, even with comfortable groans that cannot be uttered. That sweet text, Ephesians 2:13, 'Ye who sometimes were far off are made nigh by the blood of Christ', was particularly delightful and refreshing to my soul; and the more so as it reminded me of the days and months that are passed, even the day of my sensible espousals to the bridegroom of the elect. It was from that passage that Mr. Morris preached on the memorable evening of my effectual call. By the grace of God under the ministry of that dear messenger, and under that sermon, I was, I trust, brought nigh by the blood of Christ, in August 1756.

For the next two years, by Toplady's own admission, he was a devotee of the Methodists and of the theology of Wesley. It is not surprising that the pertinacious young man who had sought out famous Garrick to show him his first efforts at writing a play, also set pen to paper and wrote to John Wesley. It was the first of many letters. In a letter dated 13 September 1758, seventeen-year-old Toplady wrote his first letter to then fifty-five-year-old John Wesley, a man whose name was already well known throughout Britain. Clearly in that communication Toplady was in agreement with Wesley; it appears his Arminian leanings were what motivated him to write the letter in the first place. That was about to change.

Sovereignty prevails

'O to grace, how great a debtor', wrote Baptist hymn-writer Robert Robinson (1735–1790) in 1758, the year that young Toplady began wrestling with the doctrines of grace. Having an inquiring mind, he began carefully reading the *Thirty-*

Nine Articles of the Church of England. To his distress, he discovered that the confession of Thomas Cranmer (1489–1556) was decidedly not Arminian. Years later, Toplady would build on this initial investigation, undertaken as an Arminian, in his comprehensive work, *The Historic Proof of the Doctrinal Calvinism of the Church of England.* Toplady tells us what transpired next:

> Though awakened in 1756, I was not led into a clear and full view of all the doctrines of grace till the year 1758, when, through the great goodness of God, my Arminian prejudices received an effectual shock in reading Dr. Manton's sermons on the seventeenth chapter of St. John. I shall remember the years 1756 and 1758 with gratitude and joy in the heaven of heavens to all eternity.

This exposition by Puritan Thomas Manton (1620–1677) would have a powerful impact on the young believer, and would be the means by which he would be guided into a more thorough understanding of the free grace of God in rescuing his soul from sin and death. Imagine the effect of Manton's words on wilful, now seventeen-year-old Toplady as he read the following:

> Christ doth not take them by dozens or hundreds, but by ones and twos. Grace falls on few. Christ seeketh out the elect, if but one in a town. They were as eligible as we, only we were singled out by mere grace. The lot might have fallen upon them as well as upon you; thousands in the world were as eligible... Thy soul was as polluted as theirs, as liable to God's judgment, as deep in the same condemnation; yet such was his good-will and pleasure, to single us out.

> This is the glory of his grace: Malachi 1:2-3, 'Was not Esau Jacob's brother?' saith the Lord, 'yet I loved Jacob, and I hated Esau'. Though all men be equal in themselves, yet mercy can make a distinction. The best reason is God's good pleasure. Well, then, apply this.
>
> Look to the distinction. How many steps of election may we walk up? ... To the reason of this distinction: John 14:22, 'How is it that thou wilt manifest thyself to us, and not unto the world?' When you have searched all you can, you must rest in Christ's reason: Matthew 11:26, 'Even so, Father, for so it seemed good in thy sight'. God's supremacy over all things in heaven and in earth maketh him free to choose or refuse whom he pleaseth. It is not because you were better disposed than others; many of a better temper were passed by: God raised up a habitation to the Spirit out of crabbed knotty pieces.

Manton tested Toplady's untried theology: 'Christ seeketh out the elect, if but one in a town. They were as eligible as we, only we were singled out by mere grace.' Manton's words may have haunted him in his sleep.

Next Toplady discovered a copy of the *Confession of the Christian Religion* by Jerome Zanchius (1516–1590), published in 1562. Therein, to his youthful distress, he found still more biblical support for Calvinism. 'Up to that period', admitted Toplady, 'there was not (I confess it with abasement) a more haughty and violent free-willer within the compass of the four seas'. Looking back on his conversion and these early days of growth in grace, as Toplady seems often to have done, he wrote in 1774 an honest and specific account of the theological change that was coming over him. After one of his public blusterings about his then passionately held

Arminian soteriology, he records the impact of the gentle chiding of 'a good old gentleman':

> *One instance of my warm and ignorant zeal occurs now to my memory. About a year before the divine goodness gave me eyes to discern and a heart to embrace the truth, I was haranguing one day in company on the universality of grace and the power of free agency.*
>
> *A good old gentleman, now with God, rose from his chair, and coming to me, held me by one of my coat-buttons, while he mildly said: – 'My dear sir, there are marks of spirituality in your conversation, though tinged with an unhappy mixture of pride and self-righteousness. You have been speaking largely in favour of free-will; but from arguments let us come to experience. Do let me ask you one question, How was it with you when the Lord laid hold on you in effectual calling? Had you any hand in obtaining that grace? Nay, would you not have resisted and baffled it, if God's Spirit had left you alone in the hand of your own counsel?'*
>
> *I felt the conclusiveness of these simple but forcible interrogations more strongly than I was then willing to acknowledge. But, blessed be God, I have since been enabled to acknowledge the freeness of His grace, and to sing, what I trust will be my everlasting song, 'Not unto me, Lord, Not unto me; but unto thy name give the glory'.*

It is fitting that a man saturated with Scripture found expression to his joy in the words of the Psalmist (Psalm 115). The good old gentleman's 'simple but forcible interrogations' were used of God in the weeks that followed to awaken Toplady's understanding more fully to 'the freeness of his grace' in the gospel.

Church attendance in college

Of his remaining time at Trinity College, Dublin, Toplady gives us only fragments of information. For example, we know that he attended the Baptist meeting-house in Swift's Alley off Francis Street in Dublin, and that he developed a warm relationship with James Rutherford, pastor of the chapel. He also made friendships with Mr William Lune, Mr Manypenny, Mr Fenwick, Mr Huddleston, and others who attended the Baptist chapel.

Why Toplady, baptized and raised an Anglican, allied himself with such Nonconformists he explained with clarity. 'I was obliged either to starve my soul by never sitting under the ministry of the Word, or to go to a dissenting meeting-house. I made not a moment's hesitation in choosing the latter.' Yet he remained an Anglican. His study of the *Thirty-Nine Articles* and his new-found Calvinist theology had cemented his ecclesiological loyalties. And though preaching in the nearby Anglican Cathedral was completely devoid of the gospel, nevertheless, he would attend Holy Communion and take the Lord's Supper only at the Established church. 'And yet the clergymen at whose hands I received the memorials of Christ's dying love knew no more of the gospel than so many stocks or stones.'

College preparation

During his college years, Toplady continued writing poetry and published a short collection of it in 1759, entitled *Poems on Sacred Subjects*. Though the work reveals a sober-minded young man longing for holiness, it reveals nothing more than a hint now and then of poetic genius, as this excerpt shows:

> Shine, then, Thou all subduing light,
> The powers of darkness put to flight,
> Nor from me ever part.
> From earth to heaven be Thou my guide,
> And oh, above each gift beside,
> Give me an upright heart.

This volume of teen poetry reveals a passion for the Lord and further reveals how he occupied some of his time in college. A man of considerable academic curiosity and ability, Toplady also wrote perceptive essays on astronomy, natural philosophy, ontology, ethics, and logic.

From Toplady's diary kept in the early years of his ministry, we learn a detail that further indicates how he occupied these years of preparation in college. Writing on Sunday 27 December 1767, after a day of 'great liberty and engagement of mind' in preaching, Toplady refers specifically to a sermon he prepared during his time as a student in Dublin: 'My subject was Acts 13:39. The sermon itself (excepting a few additions here and there) was what I had formerly written in Ireland, in the year 1760, a little before I quitted college.' He then proceeded to reflect on the mercy of God for giving him gospel clarity in his theology early in life, while still a student in Dublin.

> *I can never be sufficiently thankful, that my religious principles were all fixed long before I ever entered into orders. Through the good hand of my God upon me, I set out in the ministry with clear gospel-light from the first; a*

blessing not vouchsafed to everyone. Many an evangelical minister has found himself obliged to retract and unsay what he had taught before in the days of his ignorance. Lord, how is it that I have been so signally favoured of thee! O keep me to the end steadfast in the truth. Let me but go on experimentally and sensibly to know thee; and then it will be absolutely impossible for me to depart from the precious doctrines of grace; my early insight into which I look upon as one of the distinguishing blessings of my life.

While most young people go off to college on a bacchanalian quest of self-discovery, Toplady chose the better path: he studied the Bible, wrote poetry on sacred subjects, read Puritan sermons, and prepared sermons. 'Toplady was eminently a man of one thing,' wrote Ryle. That one thing, or better yet one person, was Christ, and Toplady strained every ounce of his energy preparing himself for ordination and ministry in Christ's church.

3

ORDINATION

AND EARLY MINISTRY

In the spring of 1760, Toplady received his B. A. degree from Trinity College. After hearing one last sermon from James Morris, 'that precious man of God', nineteen-year-old Toplady and his mother boarded ship and crossed the Irish Sea to England. 'Rough passage', he recorded in his diary, dated 12 August. Mother and son finally arrived in London on 20 August. Like Augustine and his mother Monica, Toplady and his mother provide the model for how a young man who loves Christ will want to show love and honour for his mother. Often referring to her as his 'precious mother', Toplady cannot rightly be understood without appreciating the importance of her love and dedication to her son. Nor can his ministry and achievements be understood aright without recognizing her tireless ministry to him.

Anglican ordination

Perhaps as a result of taking communion from the hands of an unbelieving minister of the Church of England, who 'knew no more of the gospel than so many stocks or stones', Toplady, hereafter, seems to have developed a sense of mission, a desire to recover the Anglican Church from the sophisticated rationalism that held the church in a sort of Enlightenment head-lock. Toplady was determined to purify his church as a man working from within the ranks of its clergy.

On his first day back in London, 20 August 1760, Toplady skipped dinner and went to Tottenham Court Chapel where he heard 'dear Mr. Whitefield preach a glorious sermon'. He made the acquaintance of other leading Evangelical preachers of the day, including Revd John Gill (1697–1771), with whom Toplady may have already been in correspondence during his years at Trinity College. Gill knew of the work Toplady had done translating Zanchius's famous work on predestination — further evidence of how he spent his college years — and was now urging him to publish the work for a public readership. Young Toplady was reluctant to do so, and wrote, 'I was not then, however, sufficiently delivered from the fear of man'. Unapologetic preaching of the gospel earned a man the undying disdain of the sophisticated majority in the Anglican Church. Preach free grace and the gospel, and you were a marked man in Toplady's day. Go on record in print as a man who believes what Paul taught about predestination, and you were sure to be shuffled off to some insignificant parish in backwater England.

Through his new associations with the Evangelical party of the Anglican Church, which included George Whitefield, John Newton (1725–1807), William Romaine and others, he would eventually seek ordination as a minister in the Church of England. Why he did not join the dissenting party and seek ordination in a non-conformist congregation, Toplady, in third person, tells us himself: 'He subscribed the [Anglican] articles and liturgy from principle; and that he did not believe them merely because he subscribed them, but subscribed them because he believed them.'

A month or two before Toplady was ordained, in the spring of 1762, he was doing what his diary and letters prove to be one of his favourite activities: shopping for books. After making his purchases from 'a very respectable London bookseller', a Mr Osborne with a bookshop at Gray's Inn Gate, the man pulled young Toplady aside. Toplady gives the rest in his own words:

> He took me to the furthest end of his long shop, and said in a low voice, 'Sir, you will soon be ordained, and I suppose you have not laid in a very great stock of sermons. I can supply you with as many sets as you please, all original, very excellent ones, and they will come for a trifle'.
>
> My answer was: 'I certainly shall never be a customer to you in that way; for I am of the opinion that the man who cannot, or will not make his own sermons, is quite unfit to wear the gown. How could you think of my buying ready-made sermons? I would much sooner buy ready-made clothes'.
>
> His answer shocked me. 'Nay, young gentleman, do not be surprised at my offering you ready-made sermons, for I

*assure you I have sold ready-made sermons to many a bishop
in my time'.*

*My reply was: 'My good sir, if you have any concern for
the credit of the Church of England, never tell that news to
anybody else hence forward forever'.*

Dominated by Enlightenment ideals, the institutions
training Anglican clergy for decades had been producing
sophisticated intellectuals who cared nothing for the gospel,
including many who would become bishops. Ordination
into the Anglican clergy had become for many the path to a
life of ease, lived in proximity with the rich and influential,
dining in the first circle, and with very little work to do.
Leading worship required no original preparation; simply
read the liturgy from the *Book of Common Prayer*, and buy
'ready-made sermons'. Find a comfortable living in a quiet
parish, and your time was your own.

The deplorable condition of the state church in England
is illustrated by a story told about William Romaine, one
of Toplady's evangelical heroes in the Church of England.
Romaine was drawing so much attention for his bold gospel
proclamation that the problem was finally laid before the
king. 'Humph!' replied King George III (1738–1820). 'We
will make him a bishop; that will silence him.' The clergy in
Enlightenment England have been described as delighting
in 'women, drink, tobacco, and backgammon.' The more
respectable deistic clergy, it was said, preached an 'icy and
loveless morality'. John Newton estimated that of the 10,000
parishes in the Church of England in the eighteenth century,
9,000 had unbelieving ministers. Young Toplady was entering
a rationalist church that was a hedonistic wasteland.

Specific details of his ordination are slim, but he was first ordained an Anglican deacon in 1762 by Edward Willes (1693–1773), Bishop of Bath and Wells, who appointed the young minister to be curate of Blagdon, in the Mendip Hills of Somerset. Toplady appears to have only preached here for a period of months, certainly no more than a year.

It is while at Blagdon that Toplady penned the single hymn for which he is best known, 'Rock of Ages'. But the stories that are told of how and in what circumstances he wrote it are — though sensational — difficult to confirm or believe. The hymn and its enduring influence are worthy of more in-depth examination in later chapters.

Early fears in the pulpit

Though Toplady would never marry, he did have chaste, upright, and pastoral associations with a number of women during his thirty-eight years of ministry. Foremost among them was Lady Selina Huntingdon (1707–1791). We learn poignant details about the priorities of Toplady's early preaching ministry from a letter he later wrote to Lady Huntingdon. He admitted that in his first four years of ministry he 'dwelt chiefly on the outlines of the gospel', and he gave two primary reasons 'for thus narrowing the truths of God: I thought these points were sufficient to convey as clear an idea as was necessary of salvation. And secondly, I was partly afraid to go any further.'

> *God himself (for none but he could do it) gradually freed me*
> *from that fear. And as he never at any time permitted me*

to deliver, or even to insinuate anything contradictory to his truth, so has he been graciously pleased, for seven or eight years past, to open my mouth to make known the entire mystery of the gospel, as far as the Spirit has enlightened me into it. The consequence of my first plan of operations was, that the generality of my hearers were pleased, but only few were converted. The result of my latter deliverance from worldly wisdom and worldly fear is, that multitudes have been very angry; but the conversions which God has given me reason to hope he has wrought, have been at least three for one before. Thus I can testify, so far as I have been concerned, the usefulness of preaching predestination; or, in other words, of tracing salvation and redemption to their first source.

We are inclined to think the opposite. Preach predestination and you will have fewer converts, and your church will be small and isolated. Toplady, out of fear for his future as an Anglican minister, kept silent on predestination for the first years of his ministry. Preach things such as Thomas Manton had preached in the sermons read by teenage Toplady, and you would earn the scorn of the rationalist majority in the Church of England. Toplady knew he would be a marked man for such preaching. Paradoxically, he found that when he went to the 'first source' of redemption — an unabashed proclamation of divine grace through God's electing love in Christ — not fewer, but more people were brought to saving faith. And his church grew in numbers.

Lady Huntingdon

Toplady's letter to Lady Huntingdon brings to centre stage the role of this devout woman in eighteenth-century Christianity. No history of the Evangelical movement in England and in America would be complete without acknowledging the considerable contributions to the progress of the gospel made by Lady Huntingdon, often called the benefactress of the Evangelical movement.

Lord and Lady Huntingdon were converted at a Methodist meeting and knew John and Charles Wesley and George Whitefield personally. The first Methodist Conference was held in the Huntingdons' spacious London home. Widowed at forty-nine, Lady Huntingdon proved to be an extraordinary woman, managing considerable property and wealth while raising her seven children. Eventually she aligned herself with Whitefield's Calvinist theology and made her London drawing room a centre for his Evangelical ministry.

Lady Huntingdon often invited people of rank, the upper crust, to hear Whitefield preach in her lavishly appointed home. It is difficult for us to fully appreciate what an embarrassment her activities were to polite English society. No doubt many dukes and duchesses came under duress, hoping not to be seen. Evangelical sentiments were perceived by the elite to be at odds with the entrenched stratification of eighteenth-century society. At last one noble woman, the Duchess of Buckingham, threw caution to the wind and spoke her mind to Lady Huntingdon. Her unguarded words unmask the bigotry and arrogance of the ruling elite in Toplady's day.

I thank your Ladyship for the information concerning the Methodist preachers; their doctrines are most repulsive and strongly tinctured with impertinence and disrespect towards their superiors, in perpetually endeavouring to level all ranks, and do away with all distinctions. It is monstrous to be told, that you have a heart as sinful as the common wretches that crawl on the earth. This is highly offensive and insulting; and I cannot but wonder that your Ladyship should relish any sentiments so much at variance with high rank and good breeding.

Never cowed by her peers, Lady Huntingdon supported Evangelical preachers, especially ones within the Anglican communion like Toplady, but she also gave vast sums of money to start a ministerial training college and to build chapels, more than seventy, at a cost in today's currency values that would exceed £12,000,000 or nearly $19,000,000 US. Moreover, as a lover of music and friend and patron of George Frederick Handel, she began to see hymns and hymnals as an important part of the spread and progress of the gospel. Lady Huntingdon personally edited and selected hymns, as well as financing the publication of new hymnals.

Toplady met Lady Huntingdon while ministering to his first congregation in Blagdon in 1763. He later preached in some of her chapels, notably in Bath and in Brighton, and corresponded with her. Lady Huntingdon's activities on behalf of the Evangelical revival eventually so aggravated the rationalist Arminian majority in the Anglican Church that she was forced to break her affiliation in 1781, after which she established what was called the Lady Huntingdon's Connexion, a network of evangelical chapels throughout the realm, some of which still exist today.

Promotions and new duties

In 1764, Toplady was ordained an Anglican priest, served for a short time as curate of Farleigh Hungerford, and was eventually appointed by the bishop to pastor two congregations in Devonshire: Venn-Ottery and nearby Harpford. It was during this time that Toplady kept a regular and detailed journal of his duties, but more specifically of his communion with the Lord, his prayer life, and his ministry to his beloved flock.

What are we to make of a preacher who takes up duties at another congregation after only a few months in his first charge? We begin to wonder about a pastor whose résumé reads more like the job experience of a travelling salesman, here for a few months, there for a year, off to another position for another short stint. We begin thinking that such a pastor is probably leaving in his wake a legacy of ill-will and hard feelings. Something must be wrong with the man. But in the Anglican Church in Toplady's day, all clerical appointments were made by the bishop. Congregations had no say in who was installed to be their pastor. So Toplady's early ministry should in no way reflect poorly on him, rather on a system that did not seem to value the long-term commitment to ministry that it ought to have valued.

Another common practice in the Church of England was the practice of simony, held over from medieval Roman Catholicism, the buying and selling of church offices for money. In 1764, to his great distress, Toplady learned that some unknown individual had paid the bishop to have him appointed to Venn-Ottery and Harpford. Happy as he was in his charge, he felt compelled to resign. On Saturday 23 January 1768, he wrote that he and another minister 'made formal resignation of our respective livings... Having signed and sealed the instruments of our resignation, we left them... to be transmitted to the bishop.'

What followed may have tempted Toplady to wonder if he was not incurring Divine wrath for the resignation. He described his return from Exeter to his home in Venn-Ottery: 'The ride was far from a comfortable one. Hail, rain, or snow, almost the whole way.' It was the most remarkable weather he had ever experienced. In the waking hours of a single day, 'we have had frost and thaw, snow, rain, hail, thunder and lightning, calm, high wind, and sunshine.' Imagine the impact of such weather on the delicate health of a man with tuberculosis. But that evening, after reading a sermon by a Scottish preacher, Toplady did what he almost constantly was doing — he communed with God: 'I could look and pray to him as my covenant God in Jesus Christ, who loved me from everlasting, and will love me without end.' The theme of Christ's eternal, unchangeable love for a sinner like Toplady became the central message of his preaching ministry.

4

A PREACHING LIFE

Often referring to himself as 'the unworthiest of God's messengers', Toplady took up his preaching ministry with great seriousness, and proved to have considerable giftedness in the preaching of God's Word. Describing a season of spiritual joy and refreshment in his role as preacher, Toplady wrote, 'Duty is pleasant when God is present.'

Sprinkled generously throughout Toplady's diary are his remarks on reading the sermons of Manton, Gill, or other well-known evangelical ministers of the day. From this we may safely conclude that Toplady, though he repudiated preaching 'ready-made sermons', knew the great value of drinking deeply at both the content and the delivery of gifted preachers from the past.

Timeless advice on preaching

Toplady was soon appointed and called to Broadhembury in Devonshire, where he would minister until 1775. Before he took up his new charge, however, he wrote of an encounter that defined his preaching ministry for the remainder of his life.

Arguably one of the most valuable instructions that Toplady left for Christian ministers today is his record of a visit to Exeter and the succinct instruction he received from 'that excellent Christian, Mr. Brewer, the old ambassador of Christ'. The venerable minister recounted to young Toplady the charge he had given to another young minister in his installation service:

1. Preach Christ crucified, and dwell chiefly on the blessings resulting from his righteousness, atonement, and intercession.
2. Avoid all needless controversies in the pulpit; except it be when your subject necessarily requires it, or when the truths of God are likely to suffer by your silence.
3. When you ascend the pulpit, leave your learning behind you: endeavour to preach more to the hearts of your people than to their heads.
4. Do not affect too much oratory. Seek rather to profit than to be admired.

Toplady, who hereafter preached Christ crucified, seems to have been much impressed and affected by this wise minister's advice, and embraced the admonition as his own. What would happen if every generation of new preachers heeded these four straightforward guidelines as Toplady did? The Apostle Paul knew the danger that lurks for preachers of seeking to impress their congregation with their learning and oratory: 'For Christ did not send me to baptize but to preach the gospel, and not with words of eloquent wisdom, lest the cross of Christ be emptied of its power' (1 Corinthians 1:17, ESV).

Sermon extracts

Though only a few complete sermons of Toplady have survived, there is, nevertheless, good reason to believe that he was a skilful and persuasive preacher. His churches were often filled to capacity, with standing room only. His association with Lady Huntingdon, who asked him from time to time to preach in her chapels, further confirms his stature as a preacher among his peers. In the examples of his sermons that have survived, 'there is abundance of excellent matter', wrote Ryle, 'and a quiet, decided, knockdown, sledge-hammer style of putting things which, I can well believe, would be extremely effective'.

In 'Good News from Heaven', a sermon preached in 1774 at the Lock Chapel, Toplady earnestly cautions his hearers from coming in an unworthy manner to the Lord's Table:

Oh, beware of coming with one sentiment on your lips and another in your hearts! Take heed of saying with your mouths, 'We do not come to this thy table, O Lord, trusting in our own righteousness', while perhaps you have in some reality some secret reserves in favour of that very self-righteousness which you profess to renounce, and are thinking that Christ's merits alone will not save you unless you add something or other to make it effectual. Oh, be not so deceived! God will not thus be mocked, nor will Christ thus be insulted with impunity. Call your works what you will — the matter comes to the same point, and Christ is equally thrust out of his mediatorial throne.

Consider how Toplady understood what it meant for his people to come to the Table in a worthy manner. He wanted to make sure they were not harbouring 'some secret reserve in favour of that very self-righteousness which you profess to renounce'. He wanted to turn his people from their sins and from their good works to 'Christ's merits alone':

If you do not wholly depend on Jesus as the Lord of your righteousness — if you mix your faith in him with anything else — if the finished work of the crucified God be not alone your acknowledged anchor and foundation of acceptance with the Father, both here and ever — come to his table and receive the symbols of his body and blood at your peril! Leave your own righteousness behind you, or you have no business here. You are without the wedding garment, and God will say to you, 'Friend, how camest thou here?' If you go on, moreover, to live and die in this state of unbelief, you will be found speechless and excuseless in the day of judgment; and the slighted Saviour will say to his angels concerning you, 'Bind him hand and foot, and cast him into outer darkness ... for many are called, but few are chosen'.

Toplady was not satisfied with his people being externally moral. Preaching moralistic deism often produced outwardly upright church members. 'Leave your own righteousness behind you,' he told them. For Toplady it was mixing 'faith in him with anything else' that made someone unfit to come to Christ's Table.

Preaching with feeling

Another piece of advice Mr Brewer had taught young Toplady about preaching was to 'preach more to the hearts of your people than to their heads'. Scholar that he was, he followed this injunction. In a sermon entitled 'Free Will', preached at St. Anne's, Blackfriars, in 1774, Toplady calls his congregation to feel the truths of the gospel. Citing the *Thirty-Nine Articles* of the Anglican Church, he said that true Christians 'feel in themselves the working of the Spirit of Christ, mortifying the works of the flesh, and drawing up their minds to high and heavenly things'. He proceeded then to summarize the work of the Holy Spirit on the sinner's affections:

> Indeed, the great business of God's Spirit is to draw up and to bring down — to draw up our affections to Christ, and to bring down the unsearchable riches of grace into our hearts. The knowledge of this, and earnest desire for it, are all the feelings I plead for; and for these feelings I wish ever to plead, satisfied as I am that without some experience and enjoyment of them we cannot be happy living or dying.

Given the prevalence in our day of moralistic entertainment, all application with little or no theological truth proclaimed, too often Calvinistic preachers think they need to compensate by making little or no application. Yet again, Toplady provides a model for faithful preaching as he warmly and feelingly confronts and urges his flock:

> Let me ask you, as it were, one by one, has the Holy Spirit begun to reveal these deep things of God in your soul? If so, give him the glory of it. And as you prize communion with him, as ever you value the comforts of the Holy Ghost, endeavour to be found in God's way, even the highway of humble faith and obedient love, sitting at the feet of Christ, and imbibing those sweet sanctifying communications of

grace, which are at once an earnest of, and a preparation for complete heaven when you die.

For Toplady, there was never a dichotomy between preaching to the mind and preaching to the heart, the affections, the feelings of his people: 'God forbid that we should ever think lightly of religious feelings. If we do not in some measure feel ourselves sinners, and feel that Christ is precious, I doubt the Spirit of God has ever been savingly at work upon our souls.'

Preaching to the weak

With those words in our ears, imagine now a timorous, frail, and anxious Christian hearing these words of Toplady preached in 1770 at St. Anne's, Blackfriars (where his spiritual mentor William Romaine preached):

Faith is the eye of the soul, and the eye is said to see almost every object but itself... You may have real faith without being able to discern it. God will not despise the day of small things. Little faith goes to heaven no less than great faith; though not so comfortably, yet altogether as surely. If you come merely as a sinner to Jesus, and throw yourself, at all events, for salvation on his alone blood and righteousness, and the grace and promise of God in him, thou art as truly a believer as the most triumphant saint that ever lived. Amidst all your weakness, distresses, and temptations, remember that God will not cast out nor cast off the meanest and unworthiest soul that seeks salvation only in the name of Jesus Christ the Righteous.

If a wise preacher is the man who understands those to whom he is preaching, Toplady was a wise preacher, indeed. No one listening to Toplady's message would have scratched his head in confusion, wondering if he was justified by mostly faith but also by his works. There is never confusion in Toplady's preaching of the gospel. Careful theologian that he was, Toplady left not only his learning behind when he stepped into the pulpit, he left the terminology and the heat of controversy behind as well. But he did not leave behind his theology. Like a good poet, he adorned the doctrine and showed his congregation the loveliness of electing love and free and sovereign grace, both in justification and in sanctification:

> When you cannot follow the Rock, the Rock shall follow you, nor ever leave you for a single moment on this side of the heavenly Canaan. If you feel your absolute want of Christ, you may on all occasions and in every exigency betake yourself to the covenant love and faithfulness of God for pardon, sanctification, and safety, and with the same fullness of right and title as a traveller leans upon his own staff, or as a weary labourer throws himself upon his own bed, or as an opulent nobleman draws upon his own banker for whatever sum he wants.

As a poet preacher, Toplady was a master of figurative language, of awakening the imagination of his hearers. Notice how every metaphor is calculated to help his flock see the truth of what he proclaimed, to see with gospel clarity the sole sufficiency of the blood and righteousness of Jesus Christ. There is no mincing of words, no equivocation, no ambiguity, no erudite intimidation. Toplady preached the good news of the gospel of grace, and he did so with urgency and with authority. His flock went away filled with gospel grace, and crowded their way back with their neighbours to hear him again and again, even when he kept them 'longer than I ordinarily would have done'.

Preaching free grace and holiness

Perhaps in every generation of the church there is a lurking suspicion of preaching the free grace of the gospel. Preach the doctrines of grace and justification by faith alone, preach that sanctification is a 'work of God's free grace', and it will produce indifference to sin. But for Toplady there was never any conflict between preaching the gospel of free grace alone and Christ and him crucified and also calling himself and his congregation to live holy lives:

> *I never so feelingly wonder at my own depravity, nor so deeply abhor myself, as when the fire of divine love warms my heart, and the outpourings of God's Spirit enliven my soul. Surely the knowledge of salvation is the most powerful incentive to repentance; and not only the most prevailing, but an absolutely irresistible motive to universal holiness!*

For Toplady it was not the wrath of God, the thundering and threatening of divine judgement that produced holiness in his flock. It was the love of God and the free salvation offered and secured for sinners in the gospel that was the 'absolutely irresistible motive to universal holiness'. Here may be one of the great values of Toplady for today; he never stoops to motivate his hearers by making them think that sanctification is a condition of their justification. Also noteworthy is the fact that undergirding that preaching was prayer. Toplady never stepped into his pulpit without earnest and familiar communing and pleading with God.

5

A PRAYING LIFE

'My God, I want the inwrought prayer,' cried Toplady, 'the prayer of the heart, wrought in the soul by the Holy Ghost'. So much of the recorded praying of Toplady reflects just that, praying from the lips of a man who is filled with the Holy Spirit, whose prayers are being sanctified by the immediate presence of the God to whom he is praying. Thankfully for us, Toplady developed the habit of copying down his prayers probably as he prayed them. But there is nothing of the pompous Pharisee strutting in prayer to be seen or heard by men. His prayers are the kind of Psalm-like communing with God every Christian desires.

Distraction and wandering in prayer

Today the believer in prayer is frequently beset by distractions. And though some of our twenty-first-century distractions would have been completely foreign to Toplady, we should not fool ourselves. He was a man subject to many of the same challenges we face with prayer. 'Was afflicted with wandering in private prayer. Lord, melt down my icy heart, and grant me to wait upon thee'. Would not Toplady's confession be an accurate description of our prayer life? And like you and me, this would not be the last time he would have reason to long for greater constancy in prayer. In a diary entry dated Monday 14 December 1767, he reminds us that neglecting prayer has direct consequences:

> Before I came out of my chamber today, I was too hasty and short in private prayer. My conscience told me so at the time; and yet, such was my ingratitude and my folly, that I nevertheless restrained prayer before God. In the course of the day, I had great reason to repent of my first sin, by being permitted to fall into another.
>
> It is just, O Lord, that thou shouldest withdraw thy presence from one who waited so carelessly on thee. May I never more, on any pretext whatever, rob thee (or rather, deprive my own soul) of thy due worship; but make all things else give way to communion with thee!

Honest self-abasement

In a culture destroying itself with the cult of self-esteem, Toplady often prayed in a way that sounds foreign to our ears:

> Who am I, O Lord? The weakest and vilest of all thy called ones: not only the least of saints, but the chiefest of sinners. But though a sinner, yet sanctified, in part, by the Holy Ghost given unto me. I should wrong the work of His grace upon

my heart, were I to deny my regeneration: but, Lord, I wish
for a nearer conformity to thy image.

So unaccustomed are we to hearing someone speak of himself as 'the weakest and vilest of all thy called ones', we might be tempted to dismiss Toplady's self-deprecation as false humility. Nevertheless, Ryle concluded his study of Toplady's words in his diary by saying that we have every reason to believe them an accurate portrayal of the condition of his heart before the Lord:

My short-comings and my misdoings, my unbelief and want
of love, would sink me into the nethermost hell, was not
Jesus my righteousness and my redemption. There is no sin
which I would not commit, were not Jesus, by the power
of His Spirit, my sanctification. O when shall I resemble Him
quite, and have all the mind that was in Him? When I see Him
face to face...

Characteristically, Toplady adds at the end of this prayer, 'which God will hasten in His time'.

But this honest acknowledgment before God of his sinful condition is only half of Toplady's praying: 'At night in my chamber, God was with me in my private waiting upon him; and I could indeed say, from a heart-felt sense of his love, that it is good for me to draw nigh unto the Lord. Thy visitation, sweet Jesus, is the life and joy of my spirit.' Communing with God as Toplady so often did, he rises to ecstasies of gratitude and comfort:

Glory to thee, O Lord, for my sense of special interest in thy
everlasting love! Were all the treasures of ten thousand

worlds displayed to my view, the sight of them, the mere sight, would not make me the richer nor the happier; it is the knowledge of peculiar property in any blessing, that felicitates the soul. In this comfort lies. And, thanks to divine grace, I can look upon all the unsearchable riches of Christ, as my own. Lord, increase my faith, and add to my thankfulness more and more.

Prayer in temptation

Not only were Toplady's prayers intimate and passionate communion with God, they were theologically-informed outpourings of his heart before a God who had so mercifully distinguished him from other sinners. On 12 February 1768, after reflecting with joy on God's undeserved love for him, Toplady prayed, 'I could not long after thy presence if I did not know the sweetness of it, and love thee in some measure, and I could not know that but by a revelation of thy Spirit in my heart, nor love thee at all if thou hadst not first loved me'. But then Toplady honestly lays out for us the pride lurking in his heart. Herein is one of the authenticating marks of his diary. We should assume that, just as in the times of almost ecstatic worship and praise, he is here being equally honest as he wrestles with his sins:

I was tempted before I could get to sleep with high thoughts of my own righteousness, both as a man and as a minister. The enemy plied his fiery darts very thick, and came in as a flood, but the Spirit of the Lord lifted up a standard against him. I was enabled (glory to divine grace) to reject the cursed insinuations as I would hell-fire. Oh that ever such

*a wretch as I should be tempted to think highly of himself!
I that am, of myself, nothing but sin and weakness. I, in
whose flesh naturally dwells no good thing. I, who deserve
damnation for the best work I ever performed! Lord Jesus,
humble me to the dust, yea to the very centre of abasement
in thy presence. Root out and tear up this most poisonous,
this most accursed weed from the unworthiest heart that
ever was. Show me my utter nothingness. Keep me sensible
of my sinnership. Sink me down deeper and deeper into
penitence and self-abhorrence. Break the Dagon of pride in
pieces before the ark of thy merits. Demolish, by the breath
of thy Spirit, the walls, the Babel of self-righteousness, and
self-opinion. Level them with the trodden soil, grind them to
powder, annihilate them forever and ever. Grace, grace, be
my experience and all my cry! Amen, Amen.*

Toplady's wrestling with God in the midst of temptation
is a model for Christians when under the attack of the enemy,
especially when we are tempted to think more highly of
ourselves than we ought to think. And what Christian is not
far too often absurdly engaged in the futility of that manner
of thinking?

Joy unspeakable

Ever the humble shepherd to his flock, Toplady concluded
Sunday 2 October 1768, after a long day of prayer and
preaching, with deep gratitude that he had been called of
God to the ministry of the gospel: 'How is it, O thou God
of love, that thy tender mercies should thus accompany and
follow the vilest sinner out of hell! That, to me, who am less

than the least of all the saints, this grace should be given, that I should both experience and preach the unsearchable riches of Christ!' Toplady is a model of how our praying is enlivened when we pray God's Word back to him. Here Toplady is taking on his lips the words of the Apostle Paul (Ephesians 3), who was revelling in the immeasurable wonder of God setting him apart to preach the good news of the gospel of peace to Gentiles.

Moreover, for Toplady, prayer was not merely supplication, the kind of praying we are most inclined to. Toplady's praying is of another and higher order altogether:

> At night, before I betook myself to rest, I was enabled to act in faith very strongly on the promises. It was as if I had held a conversation with God. He assured me of his faithfulness, and I trusted him. It was whispered to my soul, 'Thou shalt find me faithful': my soul answered, 'Lord, I believe it: I take thee at thy word'. This, I am certain, was more than fancy. It was too sweet, too clear, and too powerful, to be the daughter of imagination. There was joy unspeakable, as much superior to all the sensations excited by earthly comforts, as the heavens are higher than the earth. Besides, in my experience of this kind, when under the immediate light of God's presence within, my soul is, in great measure, passive; and lies open to the beams of the Sun of Righteousness. These acts of faith, love and spiritual aspiration, are subsequent to, and occasioned by, this unutterable reception of divine influence. I bless my God, I know his inward voice; the still, small whisper of his good Spirit: and can distinguish it from every other suggestion whatever. Lord, evermore give me this bread to eat, which the world knoweth not of!

Just as Scottish Reformer John Knox (*c.*1514–1572) had 'earnest and familiar talking with God' in his life of prayer, so Toplady had enviable intimacy with the Sun of Righteousness, and is, therefore, a model for all praying neophytes, as one feels when reading the communing prayers of extraordinary Toplady.

6

A SCHOLAR'S LIFE

'It is not good for man to be alone,' God declared in the beginning, yet Toplady would never marry, never have the joy of loving companionship with his wife, would never have the pleasure of raising his own children, would have few friends and die young. Without a hint of regret, he organized his days and often his nights in the pursuit of knowledge. 'I am wedded to these pursuits as a man stipulates to take his wife, "for better, for worse, until death do us part". My thirst for knowledge is literally inexhaustible.'

In a day of high scholarship and intellectual priorities, Ryle argues that no one surpassed Toplady: 'He has never been duly appreciated. His pen seems never to have been idle.' God gave single-minded Toplady extraordinary intellectual ability and an extraordinary calling, so that, free from domestic responsibilities, he could devote himself wholly to feeding his mind so that he was better equipped to feed his flock.

Love of books

'When I get a little money I buy books,' wrote Erasmus (*c.*1466–1536) of Rotterdam. 'If there is any left I buy food and clothes.' With his memorable witticism, the Father of Renaissance Humanism encapsulated every book lover's priorities. And like Erasmus, Toplady loved books. Reading between the lines of his diary, I would say that he also loved to go shopping for them. Frequently he remarks about booksellers he visited and the particular volumes he purchased. For instance, on Friday 18 December 1767, he records, 'Rode to Honiton where I bought Whitty's *Sermons*, the excellent professor Walaeus's *Works*, and two volumes of the *Cripplegate Lectures*'.

In subsequent entries Toplady reports on the varying profit he discovered in these and many other books. 'Spent the after part of the day, reading the late Mr. Whitty's Sermons; not without some sensible comfort and joy in the Holy Ghost.' But the scholar in Toplady demanded a higher standard of copy editing from the publisher: 'Evangelical as the matter of these discourses is, the style in which they are written will not suffer me to think that the worthy author himself ever intended them for publication. It is a pity that the editor had not first let them pass under the file of some able friend.' As much as Toplady expected excellence from the book publisher's art, his love of the gospel enabled him to overlook deficiencies of form: 'The inaccuracies of composition are greatly over-balanced by the sweet savour of that precious name and adorable grace, which, to the believing soul, are as ointment poured forth.'

French Enlightenment philosophy

In another entry, Toplady offers his assessment of a French scholar's work, *Ars Critica* by Jean Le Clerc (1657–1736). The work had been 'strenuously recommended' to him by an Anglican bishop, which maybe should have tipped Toplady off. His assessment began generously: 'A most learned, and, in many respects, useful performance: yet sadly interlarded with scepticism and profaneness'. He then proceeds to an evaluation of the work, quoting extensively from both Latin and Hebrew (most editions of Toplady's diaries omit these quotations), interjecting his critique with blunt comments about the Frenchman's words, 'no more than a cold, paltry compliment, added to qualify the rudeness of what goes before'. He proceeds to dismantle Le Clerc's assertions that the Old Testament is filled with inconsistencies, that the Hebrew language itself is incomprehensible with any certainty, and that the Samarian Pentateuch was superior to the Hebrew, all mutually exclusive assertions that Toplady remarked, 'such as even I, with my little knowledge, can see through the fallacy of and refute'.

As he rounded up on his finale, Toplady seems to be throwing up his arms in despair, or is it disgust? 'Is not this the very quintessence of scepticism? And should not such a critic, with all his pomp of literature, be hissed out of the learned world?' Toplady concludes that such a man, expressing his learning in such a book, will 'sap the foundation of learning itself, and (which will always, in some measure, stand or fall with it) sound religion'. It was just such enlightened scepticism filling the halls of higher learning and the church in eighteenth-century England that prompted Toplady to cry out, 'God keep me from being a mere scholar'.

Toplady's works 'show extraordinary ability', writes Ryle. Nowhere is his scholarship more evident than in his major treatise, *Historic Proof of the Doctrinal Calvinism of the Church of England*. As logician and scholar, Toplady is given the highest accolades by Ryle:

> *It is a book that no one could have written who had not studied much, thought much, and thoroughly investigated an enormous mass of theological literature. You see at once that the author has completely digested what he has read, and is able to concentrate all his reading on every point which he handles. The best proof of the book's ability is the simple fact that down to the present day it has never been really answered. It has been reviled, sneered at, abused, and held up to scorn. But abuse is not argument. The book remains to this hour unanswered, and that for the simplest of all reasons, that it is unanswerable. It proves irrefragably, whether men like it or not, that Calvinism is the doctrine of the Church of England, and that all her leading divines, until Laud's time, were Calvinists. All this is done logically, clearly, and powerfully. No one, I venture to think, could read the book through, and not feel obliged to admit that the author was an able man.*

Though Toplady expended enormous time and energy in his controversial writings with Wesley, and though he spent a great deal of time preparing his own sermons, visiting the sick, caring for the needy in his flock, conducting services, and preaching, he somehow managed to write prodigiously and as an able scholar about many topics, and to 'write about them in a very interesting manner', wrote Ryle. He wrote well-researched and crafted biographies on three evangelical bishops, John Knox, John Foxe (1517–1587), Lord Harrington (c.1690–1756), Hermann Witsius (1636–1708), and Isaac Watts. Along with numerous essays and collected extracts from prominent Christians, Toplady also wrote scholarly observations on natural history, birds, meteors, animal behaviour (including an argument for the humane treatment of animals because they too will participate in the resurrection, a view he shared with John Wesley and others), and on the solar system. All of which reveal, according to Ryle, 'the singular activity and fertility of the author's mind … and are neither sufficiently known nor valued'.

Nevertheless, scholar that he so clearly was, Toplady heeded the advice of good old Mr. Brewer and when he stepped into the pulpit left his learning behind him. 'God keep me from being a mere scholar,' he prayed, and God heard and answered humble Toplady's prayer. The humble country folk under Toplady's pastoral care at Broadhembury never felt belittled or bullied by their pastor's learning.

7

A SHEPHERD'S LIFE

'He preached as never sure to preach again and as a dying man to dying men.' So Richard Baxter (1615–1691) wrote in *The Reformed Pastor*. Though Baxter's words were written more than fifty years before Toplady was born, they would apply to few men so well as to Toplady. To be sure, he entered the Anglican Church to preach the gospel, but equally to be a shepherd to his flock — a pastor. Though his people were largely uneducated folks from the labouring class, Toplady never referred to them in a condescending manner; his words to and about the people under his care are filled with warmth and patience, and with genuine concern for their eternal welfare. Shepherding was his goal, not impressing, and certainly not bullying.

I can think of no better way to describe Toplady's life as a pastor than for us to listen in, as it were, on his interactions with the inexhaustible variety of life that made up his country parishes. The following episodes are drawn primarily from his years of ministry in Venn-Ottery, Harpford, and Broadhembury.

A teenage thief

This morning, one William Towning, about nineteen years old, was brought here before Mr. Penny, for breaking open and robbing farmer Endicott's house yesterday afternoon, in time of service, while the family were at church. My honest parishioner, it seems, just before he went out, stepped back into his room, he knew not why, and put away a considerable sum of money into a more secret place than where it had lain for some time past; by which means he was only robbed of little more than thirty shillings in money. How evidently providential! Just before the unhappy young man was going off from Mr. Penny's to Exeter Jail, his father, who had heard of his son's situation but an hour or two before, came up to the house with a look that too plainly declared the agonies of his heart. Unable to face his parent, the young man burst into tears, and retired into the orchard, whither his guard and his father followed him.

In the era in which Toplady lived, poets often wrote occasional poems, poems inspired by a particular event and drawing a moral from the event. Toplady follows suit, but does so, not surprisingly, in humble communion with God in prayer:

Lord, if it be consistent with the counsel of thy will, be the comforter and the salvation of this sinner and his afflicted family! Bad as he is, thy grace can melt him down. By nature, I am as vile as he: yet I am, I trust, a monument of mercy, and a trophy of thy redeeming power. Blessed be the Lord, my New Creator! Blessed be the Lord, my faithful keeper!

Toplady sums up this episode with these words, 'On all occasions of this sort, I would recall that excellent line, *Aut sumus, aut fuimus, vel possumus esse, quod hic est*'. The Latin quotation is sometimes ascribed to Toplady's contemporary, Samuel Johnson, and means 'Either we are, or we have been, or may become that which is here'. Ever conscious of his own depravity, Toplady recognized that were it not for the grace of God he too would be caught in slavery to thievery or other scandalous sin. No doubt such an honest and humble posture endeared Toplady to his congregation.

The funeral of a venerable woman

From a description of teenage thievery, Toplady shifts the angle of his lens and gives us a glimpse into his pastoral ministry when preaching a funeral sermon for a dear old woman in his congregation. In a majestic sweep of events, he takes the opportunity to connect her long life to seventeenth-century history in England:

> *Sunday, February 14, 1768. In the afternoon, read prayers at Harpford, and preached Mrs. Mary Wheaton's funeral sermon, to an exceedingly great congregation indeed. I could not forbear observing, 'that God has spared her to a good old age; that she was born in the year 1675, ten years before the death of Charles II and about fourteen before the coming in of King William III; that she lived in the reigns of seven monarchs, and died last Tuesday, aged ninety-three'.*

He then describes the reaction of his people to the sermon:

Great was my fervour and enlargement of soul; nor less, to
appearance, the attention of them that heard. Nay, they
seemed to do more than attend; the word, I verily believe,
came with power and weight, to their hearts. I never yet
saw my Church so full (insomuch that there was hardly any
standing room) and, I think seldom, if ever, beheld a people
that seemed to relish the gospel better.

Toplady, who was so often ill and weary as a result of the
disease that would kill him, concluded his account of what
must have been a wearying day of ministry with, 'Neither
they nor myself were weary, though I detained them much
longer than usual.'

A drunk man under discipline

In another entry, Toplady gives us a window into the
unhappy life of ministry when a man must be brought
under the discipline of the church. Toplady did not shy
from suspending a man from the Lord's Supper, and saw
withholding the elements from a man caught in scandalous
sin as much a means of grace as partaking was for a repentant
sinner. After reading prayers and preaching, he tells us that
he began administering 'the holy sacrament':

Farmer T—e (whom I happened to meet at Miktam, no longer
ago than last Wednesday evening, so drunk that he could
hardly sit on his horse) presented himself at the Lord's table,
with the rest of the communicants; but I passed him by, not
daring to administer the symbols of my Saviour's body and
blood to one who had lately crucified him afresh, and had

*given no proof of repentance. He appeared surprised and
abashed. Lord, make this denial of the outward visible sign,
a means of inward and spiritual grace to his soul!*

Hear his pastor's heart as he prays for this discipline to be a
means of spiritual grace for the drunken man's soul. Surely
this is the way of the true pastor with his congregation.

Later he describes some of his more informal pastoral
duties with his flock: 'Drank tea at Farmer Carter's. Spent
part of the evening at Mr. Leigh's, at Hayne. Thence,
returned home — A day most intense cold.' A man riding
on horseback, and suffering with tuberculosis, particularly
notices intensely cold days.

Salvation for the dying

After receiving a letter from London from Mr. Andrew
Lacam describing the final days and death of his sister,
Toplady included the man's letter in his diary:

*She had, for some time, left the fountain of living waters.
I had two different conferences with her during her illness.
I assured her, that I did not come to lord it over her; but,
in love to her soul, put the question, 'How stand matters
between God and you?' Her attestation was, with sighs and
tears, as follows: 'I am truly sensible that I have run away
from God, and it is my heart's burden. But it is written in
God's word, "Whoso cometh unto me I will in no wise cast
out." I will, therefore, upon his promise, venture to cast my
soul, without reserve, upon Jesus Christ; and there I am sure
I can never perish.' Upon this, we went to prayer.*

Toplady's prompt and lengthy reply to the young man reveals a deep tenderness and concern for both the dying and the grieving, and for the clarity of the gospel to be further known and understood:

The account you give of dear Mrs. Carter's decease, is a ground for hope in Israel concerning her. It is a great and blessed thing when we are enabled to cast ourselves on the promises. It cannot possibly be done without faith: and he that believeth shall be saved. Adored be the free grace of God, which, I trust, healed the backslidings of your sister, and brought her again within the bond of the covenant. His Spirit alone can drive the plough-share of penitential conviction through a sinner's heart, and give us to mourn at the spiritual sight of him whom our sins have pierced. The Lord give us to mourn more and more, until we have mourned away our unbelief, our carelessness, and hardness of heart! The soul, I verily believe, is never safer than when, with returning Mary, we stand at the feet of Christ, behind him, weeping.

Toplady wanted not a single person in his congregation depending in the slightest degree for salvation on anything but on Jesus' merits in the gospel, and he demonstrated this by recording two different prayers of dying men, one humble and broken, but clinging to the God of mercy, the other presumptuous and self-righteous, hoping in his own faithfulness and obedience:

I read lately of a minister in the last century, whose departing words were, 'A broken and a contrite heart, O God, thou wilt not despise'. Nor can I think such a state to be at all inferior, in point of real safety, to that of a man who died a few years ago in London, with these triumphant words in his mouth, 'Now, angels, do your office'. Of some it is written, 'They shall come with weeping, and with supplications will I lead them;' while others of the Lord's people enter the haven of everlasting life, as it were, with full sails and flying colours: they 'return with singing unto Zion'.

Next he revels in the comfort of the eternality of 'the Father's covenant love', and the perpetual intercession of Jesus for the elect, and the faithful work of the Holy Spirit in preserving his own in faith to the end:

But this is our comfort, that of all whom the Father gave to Christ, he will not lose one. However the joy of faith may decline, the grace itself shall never totally fail; having, for its security, the Father's covenant love, which is from everlasting to everlasting; the blessed Mediator's intercession, which is perpetual and all prevailing; and the faithfulness of the Holy Ghost, who, when once given, is a fountain of living water, springing up in the believer's heart to life eternal. May he, in all his plenitude of saving grace and heavenly love, descend upon our souls as dew, and make us glad with the light of his countenance!

Imagine the comfort the following words would have brought to his humble flock. 'He never forsakes the sinner he has loved', and 'he has engaged that the regenerate soul shall never totally forsake him, else there would never be a saint in heaven':

When I consider the goodness of God to me, the chief of sinners, I am astonished at the coldness of my gratitude and the smallness of my love. Yet, little and cold as it is, even that is his gift, and the work of his Spirit. An earnest, I cannot doubt, of more and greater. The Lord Jesus increase the spark to a flame, and make the little one become a thousand! My health, after which you are so kind as to enquire, was never better. And, which is greater still, I often experience the peace that passeth all understanding, and the joy that is unspeakable and full of glory. Not that I am always upon the mount. There are seasons, in which my Lord is 'as one that hideth himself'. But he only hides himself. He never forsakes the sinner he has loved. And, blessed be his name, he has engaged that the regenerate soul shall never totally forsake him; else, there would never be a saint in heaven.

Giant of learning, of theology, of spiritual devotion that Toplady was, he always identified himself with the weakest among his flock:

I rejoice to hear of Mrs. W's temporal welfare; and pray God to make her, spiritually, such as he would have her to be. She and I have much chaff to be burnt up; much tin to be consumed; may the blood of the Lamb be upon us both, for pardon; and the sacred Spirit be to us as a refining fire, for sanctification.

And observe how careful Toplady is to disabuse his people of any relying upon themselves in salvation. To make his point more vividly, he marshals appropriate metaphors as a poet would do:

If you write to her, do present the captain and her with my Christian respects: and let her know from me, that except she comes to Christ as a poor sinner, with the halter of self-abasement round her neck, and the empty vessel of faith in her hand; as a condemned criminal, who has nothing to plead; and as an insolvent debtor, who has nothing to pay; she is stout-hearted, and far from righteousness. The way to be filled with the fullness of God, is to bring no money in our sack's mouth. If you see my old friend, Mr. I. tell him, that he will not be able to find any rest for the sole of his foot, until he returns to the doctrines of grace, and flies back to the ark of God's election.

Reading this string of rich metaphors from Toplady's pen makes me feel that he may be about to break into writing a hymn. One must come to Christ 'with the halter of self-abasement ... the empty vessel of faith ... as a condemned criminal', bringing 'no money in our sack's mouth' and flying 'back to the ark of God's election'. Only the deeply-informed theologian who is also a gifted poet can order his words with this kind of force and beauty.

Widows, farmers and the poor

Toplady described a church dinner where, though there were many people gathered to share the tithe meal, he had 'several opportunities of conversing on the best subjects, particularly the decrees of God, and the spiritual impotence of man's will'. We next get a window into parish life in Broadhembury, life made up of elderly folks, poor farmers, and widows in need of support from the church:

Paid farmer Carter for four bushels of wheat, to be distributed among the poor, as follows: John Churchill, Robert Bishop, Henry Wilson, James Bedford, Jr., Joseph Wescoat, James Wey, Sarah Hare, John Churchill of Southertown, Charles Redwood, Patience Hall, William Perry, William May, Jr., Elias Tews, Richard Haddon, and Richard House, one peck each; and half a peck each to Elizabeth Critchard, and William May, Sr.

Toplady gives us many brief glimpses of his flock and ministry, and in all of them he constantly returns to his chief concern and delight. After one sermon he wrote, 'a spirit of great earnestness and life appears to have been poured out on my people'. When leaving one congregation for another (due to the bewildering machinations of Anglican hierarchy) he prayed for the Lord's presence to go with him, and asked his Heavenly Father to 'Take care of thy own elect (and so thou assuredly wilt) here and in this neighbourhood!'

After meeting with a man who travelled some distance to church, Toplady wrote,

Mr. Holmes, of Exeter, came thence this morning to hear the unworthiest of God's messengers. This gentleman was at my churches both parts of the day; and, from what conversation I had with him, appears to be one who knows and loves the truth as it is in Jesus.

After preaching to his attentive flock at Broadhembury, Toplady described his impressions of his hearers and a few moments of good conversation over coffee at the vicarage after the service:

Wet as the afternoon has proved, a great number of strangers were at church; and, I verily think, the presence and power of God were amongst us. After service good old Mrs. Hutchings, and Joan Venn, drank coffee with me at the vicarage. Our conversation was, for the most part, savoury and comfortable. Was rejoiced to hear, that the word of God from my lips has been greatly blessed of late, to those two persons; to Farmer Copp, and his eldest son; to old Mr. Thomas Granger, Farmer Smith, and several other of my parishioners. Since I came down last into Devonshire from London, God has owned my ministry more than ever.

We are not surprised when Toplady concludes his reflections on these evidences of God's blessing on his ministry by communing with God in a prayer of heartfelt gratitude. 'Blessed Lord, the work is thine alone: go on, I most humbly beseech thee, to speak to the hearts of sinners, by the meanest mouth that ever blew the trumpet in Zion!' His public duties completed, he gives us a picture of the bachelor pastor spending the Lord's Day evening (the second service on Sunday was always in the afternoon) curled up with a good book. 'At night, I was much comforted in spirit, in reading Bishop Beveridge's *Private Thoughts*.'

The unmarried pastor and a female parisihoner

Bachelor Toplady had a chaste relationship with Lady Huntingdon and with several other women in his congregation and his extended circle of acquaintances. His record of the written testimony of one dear woman in his flock, a Joan Venn, puts to rest the suggestions of inappropriate behaviour some moderns clamour to find in Toplady's relationship with women under his pastoral care. She wrote to her pastor an 'account of God's past dealings with her soul':

> I have had very deep thought, and very great trouble, since my last discourse with you. I have looked into my life past; I have ransacked my soul; and called to mind the sinful failings of my youth: and I find it very hard and difficult, to make my calling and election sure.
>
> I have earnestly desired to leave no corner of my soul unsearched; and I find myself a grievous and wretched sinner. I have committed grievous sins, very grievous sins, such sins as are not fit to be named before God's saints. I have examined my soul by each particular commandment, and find myself guilty of the breach of all, and that in a high degree. And now, when I look upon the glass of the law, and there see my own vileness, I find God's justice and my own deserts even ready to surprise me and cast me down into the nethermost hell and that most righteously; but O see the goodness of a gracious God, in that he hath given me a sight of my sins! And I am inclined to think, that, if God did not work with me, this sorrow could not be.
>
> O, sir, I cannot but let you know, that sometimes I have some blessed thought of God; and O, how sweet are they to my soul! They are so ravishing, that I cannot possibly declare it; but they are like the morning cloud and early dew, soon gone, and then I am afraid. I have had abundance of trials and temptations in these three years almost; but if I could think that my dear Lord had shed his blood for me, I should

not be so much shaken; and, because I cannot apply these
things to myself, my heart doth mourn with me. I am greatly
afraid of the deceitfulness of my heart, lest that should
deceive me. But let the righteous smite me, and it shall be a
kindness; and let him reprove me, and it shall be excellent oil
which shall not break my head.

O, that the Lord Jesus Christ would now sprinkle what I
have said with his precious blood! And, now I have opened
my soul to you, I most humbly beg and desire your advice
concerning these weighty matters; for they are matters
which concern my never dying soul. And I have a high esteem
for you: but what is my esteem? The esteem of a poor worm,
of a poor sinful creature. O that the Lord would let me see,
more and more, my own vileness! Now I have declared to
you what the Lord, through grace, hath revealed to me;
though I am unworthy to write to such.

Toplady's response to Joan Venn's letter? 'O, that all my
parishioners were, not only almost, but altogether such, in
spirit, as this woman! Illiterate she is, and, I believe, chiefly
supports herself by spinning: but, when God teaches, souls
are taught indeed.' Yet, she appears much less illiterate than
Toplady gives her credit for and sounds very much as if she
has been intently listening and taking to heart her pastor's
ministry to her.

An unrepentant farmer

Imagine a man of intelligence and learning, educated in
prestigious institutions, a noted scholar, imagine him the

pastor of a country parish filled largely with uneducated
working-class folks. And then one of the members of his
congregation, who had recently travelled to London, handed
him after services two London newspapers. Without
internet, television, instant news with the click of the mouse,
Toplady may have received these as a man lost in the desert
receives a flask of cold water. But it was the Sabbath, and
Toplady set them aside. 'I hope to read [them] tomorrow but
dare not do so on God's day.'

The same man brought him 'a letter from my honoured
mother', which he no doubt looked forward to reading that
evening after his duties were done for the day. But, pastor
that he was, his flock came first. An old man was calling for
the minister to come to his home. Toplady went:

> After evening service, visited and prayed with William May
> Sr. His cry was, 'What shall I do to be saved?' But I could not,
> on close conversation with him, discover the least sign of
> evangelical repentance. He neither sees the vileness of his
> heart, nor knows his need of Christ. Lord, bless what I was
> enabled to speak, and do that work upon his soul which man
> cannot!

Listen in to honest pastors speaking with one another
about their ministry and one will hear of difficulties and
discouragements. Toplady was not immune from these:

> One of the most difficult and discouraging parts of the
> ministry, I have long found, is visiting the ignorant and
> unawakened sick. But nothing is too hard for God. He, whose
> grace wrought on me, is able to work on the sinner I have

been with to-day; and will assuredly, if his name is in the Book of Life.

Toplady's theology was eminently a practical theology. His only hope for the 'ignorant and unawakened sick' was 'the rock of God's eternal election':

Amidst all our discouragements, in ministering to others; and amidst all our doubts respecting ourselves; there is yet a foundation both sure and steadfast, even the rock of God's eternal election. Was it not for this, how would my hands hang down! and what hope could I have for myself or others? But this sets all to rights. The unchangeable Jehovah knows His own people by name, and will, at the appointed season, lead them, out of a state of nature into a state of grace, by effectual vocation: for 'whom He did predestinate, them He also called'. This is all my salvation, and all my desire: the ground of the former, and the object of the latter.

So, after a long exhausting day of ministry in the pulpit, in prayer, and in the home of a sick old man who remained hardened in his unbelief, Toplady concluded the weary day in sweet and joyful communion with the ever-present Christ:

At night, God is very gracious to me in secret prayer. Great was my joy in the Lord; sweet my communion, and free my access. O that I had something to render Him for all His benefits! Just before I went to bed, that blessed promise was whispered powerfully to my soul, and sensibly sealed upon my heart, 'I will never leave thee, nor forsake thee.' Amen. Lord Jesus.

As pastor and shepherd Toplady ministered so effectively because he knew who he was: 'a dying man' ministering 'to dying men'. Though his pastoral ministry was always and ever deeply theological, never did Toplady bring the verbiage of that theological controversy for which he is known into that ministry. Nevertheless, in a day when the doctrines of grace were most under assault by the rationalists and moralists in the church, Toplady was called to contend for the doctrine of God's eternal and gracious predestination.

8

A CONTENDING LIFE

In 1775, Toplady's declining health required him to suspend his duties in Broadhembury and seek relief in a different climate and perhaps under the care of a different physician. He spent his final three years in London preaching in a French Calvinist chapel in Orange Street. One day on the street in London a critic of the doctrine of predestination recognized Toplady and accosted him. He records the encounter in a letter written on 6 April 1775. 'Would you, if you were God,' said his accuser, 'create any being to misery?' Toplady replied, 'When I am God, I will tell you'! For many the sum total of Toplady's life is that he was a young hothead who had the insolence to take on the theology of the venerable John Wesley and to say mean things about the saintly man. This, I hope to show, is a grossly unfair reduction of Toplady and of the actual events that transpired in the theological controversy between Wesley and Toplady.

Battle lines drawn

Toplady's contemporary and fellow hymn-writer John Byrom (1692–1763) fell decidedly against Toplady and Whitefield on the Arminian side of the theological debate. Byrom is remembered for a Christmas carol written in 1749 for his daughter Dolly, who, when asked what she wanted for Christmas, requested a Christmas poem. Her father gave her and the world, 'Christians, Awake, Salute the Happy Morn'. Byrom would have done well to stick to Christmas carols, but he also wrote doggerel verse as he weighed in on the controversy:

> Flatter me not with your Predestination,
> Nor sink my spirits with your Reprobation.

Byrom ironically claimed to distance himself from the entire dispute, yet reserved all his mockery for the Calvinists, whose theological view, he concluded, 'contradicts all gospel and good sense'.

Entering the fray

Toplady first entered the fray of controversy in 1769 when six young Oxford students were expelled from St. Edmund Hall for their embrace of historic Reformed Christianity. The six young men were expelled ostensibly because their views were inconsistent with the teaching of the Church of England. This was too much for Toplady. Recall that he had in 1758 nearly rejected the Church of England precisely *because* the *Thirty-Nine Articles* were Calvinist. Though he had previously feared publishing his translation of Zanchius's work on predestination, the time was clearly ripe. Toplady published his translation of Zanchius's *Confession of the Christian Religion* (1562), entitling his translation *The Doctrine of Absolute Predestination Stated and Asserted*. John Wesley got hold of it, and the debate was on.

Pamphlets flew back and forth for the next five years. In 1774, Toplady completed and published a remarkable 700-page volume proving that the leading lights of the Church of England had taught predestination since its beginning. According to Ryle, Toplady's tome, though often scorned, has never been refuted because it is unanswerable.

In the controversy with Wesley, young Toplady often gets tarred as the harsh, vitriolic pot-stirrer. Even a cursory examination of the evidence, however, suggests otherwise. In response to Toplady's translation of Zanchius's work on predestination, Wesley took an unethical course of action that set a vicious tone for the debate. Wesley issued an edition of Toplady's translation, heavily edited and altered, but still bearing Toplady's name. Wesley's version concluded:

> *The sum of all is this: One in twenty of mankind are elected; nineteen in twenty are reprobated. The elect shall be saved, do what they will; the reprobate will be damned, do what they can. Reader believe this, or be damned. Witness my hand.*

The Wesley modified edition left the reader no option but to conclude that this statement was Toplady's, and an accurate summation of his (and Zanchius's) teaching on predestination. Some still think so today. Nothing could be further from the truth. The words were not Toplady's;

they were Wesley's caricature borne out of his opposition to predestination.

Toplady responded by writing, *A Letter to the Rev Mr. John Wesley; Relative to His Pretended Abridgement of Zanchius on Predestination.* He confronted the elder Wesley: 'Why did you not abridge me faithfully and fairly? Why must you lard your ridiculous compendium with additions and interpolations of your own; especially as you took the liberty of prefixing my name to it?' One Wesleyan biographer admitted that thirty-year-old Toplady had the evidence on his side. For his slander of Toplady, sixty-seven-year-old Wesley must take responsibility for muddying the debate. Toplady continued: 'Are these the weapons of your warfare? Is this bearing down those who differ from you with meekness? Do you call this binding with the cords of love? Away, for shame, with such disingenuous artifices.' Toplady went on:

> By what spirit this gentleman and his deputies are guided in their discussion of controversial subjects, shall appear from a specimen of the horrible aspersions which, in 'The Church Vindicated from Predestination', they venture to heap on the Almighty Himself. The recital makes one tremble; the perusal must shock every reader who is not steeled to all reverence for the Supreme Being. Wesley and Sallon are not afraid to declare that on the hypothesis of divine decrees, the justice of God is no better than the tyranny of Tiberius. That God Himself is 'little better than Moloch'. 'A cruel, unwise, unjust, arbitrary, a self-willed tyrant'. 'A being devoid of wisdom, justice, mercy, holiness, and truth'. 'A devil, yea, worse than the devil'. Did the exorbitancies of the ancient Ranters, or the impieties of any modern blasphemers, ever come up to

this? ... Observe, reader, that these also are the very men who are so abandoned to all sense of shame, as to charge me with blasphemy for asserting with Scripture, that God worketh all things according to the counsel of His own will, and that whatever God wills is right. 'Being predestinated according to the purpose of him who worketh all things after the counsel of his own will' (Ephesians 1:11).

How did Wesley respond to this? In a condescending letter dated 24 June 1770, Wesley famously replied: 'I do not fight with chimney-sweepers. He is too dirty a writer for me to meddle with. I should only foul my fingers.'

Toplady also proceeded to accuse Wesley of plagiarism. But he was quick to clarify that his response was not one of personal animosity. 'Let it not be supposed that I bear [Wesley] the least degree of personal hatred,' he wrote. 'God forbid. I have not so learned Christ. The very men who have my opposition have my prayers also.' As a scholar and theologian, Toplady supported his accusation with irrefutable evidence of plagiarism, but not only in Wesley's altered revision of Toplady's work. In Wesley's *Calm Address*, wherein he criticized the American colonists for their rebellion, Wesley had included numerous passages from Samuel Johnson's *Taxation No Tyranny*, but made no mention of his name, representing the words of the famous 'Dictionary Johnson' as his own. Wesley was called to answer for this by others besides Toplady and was forced to make some semblance of an apology for it; he did give Johnson credit in a later edition.

The ball was in Wesley's court. Refusing to reply directly to Toplady, Wesley issued a highly edited version of the Canons of Dordt that further fuelled Toplady's outrage at the man's methods. Wesley seems to have had little compunction about altering documents and adding to them, yet representing them to the public as the unaltered original. In a textbook case of building a straw-man argument, Wesley published his truncated Canons of Dordt, representing his revision as the official seventeenth-century theological document. His revised and baldly condensed edition significantly left out, among other things, the biblical quotations used to support predestination. Armed with his altered version of Dordt, Wesley succeeded in making eternal election sound harsh, unfeeling, and wholly out of character with the love and grace of God. Toplady felt compelled to reply to yet another outrageous misrepresentation of Christian theology, but he did so with some measure of caution:

> Much as I disapprove Mr. Wesley's distinguishing principles, and the low cunning with which he circulates them, I still bear not the least ill will to his person. As an individual, I wish him well, both here and ever… I make, however, no scruple to acknowledge that manuscript of the following sheets has lain by me some weeks, merely with a view of striking out from time to time, whatever might savour of undue asperity and intemperate warmth.

Ryle wishes, and rightly so, that Toplady had lain more of his words by and not taken them up until he could do so with more graciousness. He bemoans that some of 'the epithets he applies to his adversaries are perfectly amazing and astonishing'. Unlike defenders of Wesley, however, Ryle goes on to say, 'It must in fairness be remembered that the language of [Toplady's] opponents was exceedingly violent, and was enough to provoke any man.' We live in a world that likes to think of itself as kinder and gentler, but it is a world where politeness of speech is often valued more highly than accuracy of speech. 'Men were perhaps more honest and outspoken than they are now,' observed Ryle.

Provoked and wronged as Toplady was by Wesley, one wonders what would have happened if the former had taken his Saviour's approach and when reviled had not reviled in return. Though he was not referring to Toplady or Wesley specifically, John Newton encapsulated the danger men face when engaged in controversy over things they care deeply about. 'There is a principle of self, which disposes us to despise those who differ from us; and we are often under its influence, when we think we are only showing a becoming zeal in the cause of God.'

Who was right?

Few men are at their best in controversy, and Toplady was no exception. After lamenting Toplady's vitriol and harshness in his condemnation of Wesley's underhanded and unethical methods, Ryle wrote without equivocation that Toplady's theology was 'scriptural, sound, and true'. We may rightly cringe at the tone of some of his verbal salvos, but when the dust settles and the shouting has died down, we must get down to the serious business of deciding whether Toplady got things right or not. Ryle was convinced that he did:

I will never shrink from saying that the cause for which Toplady contended all his life was decidedly the cause of God's truth. He was a bold defender of Calvinistic views about election, predestination, perseverance, human impotency, and irresistible grace. On all these subjects I hold firmly that Calvin's theology is much more scriptural than the theology of Arminius. In a word, I believe that Calvinistic divinity is the divinity of the Bible, of Augustine, and of the Thirty-Nine Articles of my own Church, and of the Scots Confession of Faith.

Toplady came down on the side of the free grace of God and soundly against the perfectionism and man-centred theology that was eroding and replacing the good news in his day. 'Well would it be for the Churches', wrote Ryle, 'if we had a good deal more men of clear, distinct, sharply-cut doctrine in the present day! Vagueness and indistinctness are marks of our degenerate condition.' Toplady bent every theological nerve to stand fast against the doctrinal degeneracy of his day and to proclaim with clarity unwavering doctrinal truth.

The controversy in perspective

Toplady took a stand for the gospel. Yes, there was bungling on his part, but he took his stand, and did so for the gospel's sake. Perhaps Toplady's intrepid stand for truth will inspire Christians in this generation to stand fast for the gospel's sake — come what may. And how much better if they also learn from Toplady's sometimes contentious spirit, and lament the errors of others with tears, and by adorning the truth with Christ-like love and gentleness cause our enemies to be won over to the truth.

Now, there is one place where Toplady's contending for the faith once delivered to the saints is free from any hint of bitterness and that is in his hymns.

9

A PRAISING LIFE

'Really good hymns are exceedingly rare,' wrote Ryle. 'There are only a few men in any age who can write them.' For Ryle, Toplady was one of those few. But what makes a hymn a great hymn? What qualities make a hymn capture the spiritual imagination of generations of Christians? Perhaps more to the point, what qualities make a hymn-writer able to craft such a hymn?

Hymnologist Thomas Wright gives an evocative description of the sweat and blood that goes into penning the finest hymns. The poet is not first and foremost concerned with niceties of style, and witty turns of phrase. Caught up with devotional fervour, the hymn-writer is compared with Bunyan's Pilgrim in mortal combat with the fiend:

> The writer seeks to express his devotional fever, and succeeds [when, he, like] Christian is in deadly strife with Apollyon, when darts fly thick, and the ground is slippery with scales, blood and spume, his chief thought is not whether the coat on his back is of the latest cut from Paris. Indeed he is so busy

with his adversary that he does not know whether he has a
coat or a back either. In a quieter moment he can polish his
stanza, that is if his stanza admits of polish; but he will in no
case sacrifice his original meaning, or weaken even so little
as a single line, just for the purpose of tickling the foolish ear
of the peddler or the dilettante.

Though it is impossible to know precisely whether Toplady experienced this kind of violent 'blood and spume' as he wrote 'Rock of Ages', there are clear evidences in the hymn itself of the unction and brilliance that must have animated its author when he wrote it.

Rock of Ages

'The most popular hymn in the English language', wrote hymnologist Francis Arthur Jones in 1903 of Toplady's 'Rock of Ages'. But as with popular things they sometimes get tampered with. There is a persistent, though highly unlikely, story behind the writing of this hymn. The story appeared in the *London Times* in the late nineteenth century in an account given by Sir William Henry Wills, landowner in Blagdon:

Toplady was one day overtaken by a heavy thunderstorm in
Burrington Coombe, on the edge of my property (Blagdon),
a rocky glen running up into the heart of the Mendip range,
and there, taking shelter between two massive pillars of our
native limestone, he penned the hymn, Rock of Ages, Cleft
for Me.

This often-repeated story has been ornamented and expanded to include Toplady casting about for something on which to write the lines as they came to him. Finding no paper in his pockets, he resorted to scouring the dirt floor of the cleft into which he had hidden himself for shelter. The manufacturers of hymn stories could not pass up the ironies: Toplady discovered at his feet a playing card apparently dropped by a previous — and more vulgar — shelterer in the cleft. The tale has him hastily write down the hymn on the card. One sceptic insists that there are a number of American libraries and museums who have on display the original playing card with Toplady's first draft written on it, suggesting rather strongly that it is the American love of sentimentality and sensationalism that fuels such hymnological fabrications.

What is known to be true is that in 1775, twelve years after the episode when Toplady took refuge from a storm in the crags of Burrington Coombe, and just three years before his death, Toplady's famous hymn was first published in the *Gospel Magazine*. It was reprinted the next year in a collection of hymns compiled by Toplady.

Holiest believer in the world

Hymn XXIII in Toplady's *Psalms and Hymns* bears the heading, 'A living and dying prayer for the holiest believer in the world.' We might blanch when we first read the title Toplady gave the hymn. Is he referring to himself as the 'holiest believer in the world'? Doesn't that seem a bit arrogant? Or is this a shot at Wesley, a thumbing-the-nose at his perfectionism? But when we connect the title with the theological substance undergirding the poetry, misunderstanding dissolves.

Toplady, who often wrote, 'I am worse than nothing for I am a vile sinner', could not have been preening his own righteousness here. But in one sense it was a jab at Wesley's perfectionism. 'Nothing in my hand I bring', wrote Toplady. 'Simply to thy cross I cling.' Here is seen the eminently practical character of Toplady's Calvinism. It was Christ's imputed righteousness alone that made him the 'holiest believer in the world', and nothing else. Clearly it was the alien righteousness of Jesus to which Toplady referred in the title, and, as he had argued with Wesley, his own imagined righteousness is filthy rags in God's sight. And for Toplady what was true in justification was equally true in sanctification.

Ironically, the doctrine of imputed righteousness is adorned in a near perfect poetic conjunction by both Toplady and Wesley. The year Toplady was born, 1740, Wesley translated and versified a marvellous hymn of Ludwig von Zinzendorf's 'Jesus, Thy Blood and Righteousness'. I cannot imagine a single phrase in that hymn that expresses a theology with which Toplady would not have wholeheartedly agreed. When crafting a hymn to sing in worship, Wesley seemed compelled to lay aside his syncretism. Wesley wrote that on the resurrection day, when standing before the glory of God in heaven, 'This shall be all my plea, Jesus hath lived, hath died for me' — perfectly expressing the Calvinist doctrine of the active and passive obedience of Christ for sinners.

National debt and grace

A satirical essay Toplady wrote in 1775 not only gives us insight into his wit and into the mounting taxation crisis in the American colonies, but it provides us with perspective on his most enduring hymn. Toplady entitled the essay 'Questions and answers relative to the National Debt'. Royal squandering and the debilitating price tag and territorial losses of The Seven Years' War (1754–1763) had left Britain teetering on the brink of financial disaster. The national debt was headline news, as anyone living in today's world can appreciate.

Just as economists attempt to help us get our minds around the number of £100 notes it takes to make a trillion pounds, Toplady attempted to help readers visualize just how vast England's debt was by describing how long it would take a man counting 100 shillings an hour to count the debt. If he did nothing else but count shillings throughout his life, the counter would have to live ninety-eight years, 316 days, fourteen hours and forty minutes — and no stopping to eat or sleep.

Toplady was just getting warmed up. He went on to calculate the weight of a shilling and then what 2,600,000,000 shillings weighed. Then he calculated how much weight an oxcart could carry and concluded it would require 20,968 carts to transport the debt. Next he figured out how far two-and-a-half billion shillings would stretch around the globe if laid side by side, and then how much interest it cost England to maintain such enormous debt. He finally concluded that there was not enough money in all Europe to pay off the debt. Some things never change.

But Toplady was not merely engaged in a witty exercise in economic and political satire. The enormity of the national debt, for Toplady, provided an elaborate metaphor for explaining the gospel of grace. Just as it was impossible for England to pay her financial debt, Toplady proceeded to show how impossible it is for us to pay our sin debt to God.

He calculated how great the debt of sin owed to God is if a person sinned once in twenty-four hours, twice in a day, once an hour, once a minute, and finally once every second. He estimated that if a man lived eighty years (Toplady would live only thirty-eight years) and committed one sin per second, a person would be indebted to God for a total of 2,522,880,000 sins. Toplady concluded that each of us is hopelessly lost because of our enormous debt of sin — lost beyond recovery and destined to pay our own debt for all eternity in hell.

Unshakeable foundation

Following on the reasoning in his essay on debt, Toplady published 'Rock of Ages' in 1776 in a collection of sacred poetry entitled *Psalms and Hymns*. Intensely personal and filled with evocative imagery, little could Toplady have known that it would become one of the greatest hymns in the English language:

> Rock of Ages, cleft for me
> Let me hide myself in thee;
> Let the water and the blood,
> From thy riven side which flowed,
> Be of sin the double cure;
> Cleanse me from its guilt and power.

Toplady may have drawn the language of the hymn from Isaiah 26:4, which could be translated 'Trust in the LORD forever, for the LORD God is an everlasting rock' (ESV). Toplady would have been conversant with other biblical imagery of this kind: God gave Israel water in the wilderness when Moses struck a rock; God hid Moses in the cleft of a rock when God's glory passed by; later, the Apostle Paul explains that Christ is the spiritual Rock, the firm foundation and the only refuge for lost sinners.

> Not the labour of my hands
> Can fulfil thy law's demands;
> Could my zeal no respite know,
> Could my tears forever flow,
> All for sin could not atone;
> Thou must save, and thou alone.

In one of his polemic works, Toplady had ably argued that Wesley's Arminianism and perfectionism led inexorably back to the works righteousness taught by the Roman Catholic Church. With Pauline clarity and Psalm-like skill, Toplady adorned the doctrine of man's total inability to meet the perfect requirement of God's holy law: 'Not the labour of my hands /Can fulfil thy law's demands'. No amount of well-intentioned zeal, no endlessly-flowing tears of regret could save the sinner: 'Thou must save, and thou alone'. Toplady would be the first to admit that there was nothing theologically innovative here, though there is masterful poetic originality in how he expressed these timeless truths of the gospel.

> Nothing in my hand I bring,
> Simply to thy cross I cling;
> Naked, come to thee for dress;
> Helpless, look to thee for grace;
> Foul, I to the fountain fly;
> Wash me, Saviour, or I die.

Just as in his preaching Toplady kept Christ and his cross at the centre of his message, so in his poetry he held high the cross of the Saviour. Nothing else would do to satisfy the enormous debt the sinner owes.

> While I draw this fleeting breath,
> When my eyelids close in death,*
> When I soar to worlds unknown,
> See thee on thy judgment throne,
> Rock of Ages, cleft for me,
> Let me hide myself in thee.

* Here is an example of hymnal editors improving on the original. What Toplady actually wrote was 'When my eye-strings break in death'.

In words penned by a pastor who preached 'as a dying man to dying men', here Toplady adorns the sinner's hope when facing death and soaring 'to worlds unknown'. When the sinner stands before the judgement bar of God, he will not look to 'the labours of [his] hands', or to his all-too-pathetic faithfulness, or to his partial obedience. He will hide himself in the atoning sacrifice and perfect righteousness of Jesus Christ alone. Because our sins are so great, there is absolutely nothing we can do to fulfil God's holy demands. But God sent his beloved Son to do for us what we could not do for ourselves.

Influence of 'Rock of Ages'

It has been said that 'No other English hymn can be named which has laid so broad and firm a grasp upon the English-

speaking world' as Toplady's 'Rock of Ages'. An illustration
of this occurred early in 1892, as Albert Victor, grandson
of Queen Victoria, lay dying of influenza. It is told that he
recited 'Rock of Ages, Cleft for me' on his deathbed. 'For if in
this hour', he reportedly said, 'I had only my worldly honours
and dignities to depend upon, I should be poor indeed'.

Hymnologist W. T. Stead, in his volume *Hymns That
Have Helped*, records that when the steamer *London* went
down in the Bay of Biscay, 11 January 1866, the last boatload
of people rescued from the ship said they heard the doomed
passengers singing 'Rock of Ages' as the vessel sank.

Another revealing story about the hymn is told of a
nineteenth-century missionary in India eager to spread the
good news of the gospel of free grace to the predominantly
Hindu population. Certain that 'Rock of Ages, Cleft for
Me' would provide imagery the native population could
grasp, the zealous missionary hired a native Hindu student
to translate Toplady's hymn into Sanskrit. When the work
was completed, the missionary eagerly translated the Hindu
student's version back into English to see how the hymn had
fared in the translation. Imagine his disappointment when
he read the opening lines:

Very old stone, split for my benefit,
Let me absent myself under one of your fragments.

Poet physician Elliot Emanuel observed that 'poetry is
what eludes translation'. The young missionary discovered
that though original truths may be translated, the imagery
and subtle nuances of language are entirely another matter.

Ironically, Toplady's 'Rock of Ages' even made its way
into Wesleyan hymnals, but usually with the poet's name

'relegated to decent obscurity in out-of-the-way indexes', as Bernard L. Manning puts it. This practice, alas, also served to confuse the origin of some hymns. Some Methodists and critics of Toplady still maintain that Toplady plagiarized 'Rock of Ages' from their founder, John Wesley, though I can find nothing more than ignorance or envious partisanship to support this claim.

Another evidence of the enduring nature of Toplady's finest hymn takes place weekly in his hometown. In honour of one of its greatest sons, every evening worship service at St. Andrew's Parish Church, Farnham, where Toplady was baptized, fittingly concludes with the singing of a stanza from 'Rock of Ages'.

Extravagant praise

Lamenting that Toplady did not live longer, write more hymns and engage in fewer controversies, Ryle ranks Toplady as one of the greatest of English hymn-writers: 'I give it as my decided opinion that he was one of the best hymn-writers in the English language. I am quite aware that this may seem extravagant praise; but I speak deliberately. I hold that there are no hymns better than his.' The great evangelical Anglican bishop of the nineteenth century proceeds to explain more precisely his reasons for saying this. 'Of all English hymn-writers, none, perhaps, have succeeded so thoroughly in combining truth, poetry, life, warmth, fire, depth, solemnity, and unction, as Toplady has.'

10

A DEBTOR'S LIFE

'Truth, poetry, life, warmth, fire, depth, solemnity, and unction.' Perhaps in these words Ryle has given us one of the most succinct and precise definitions of what a hymn actually is. Yet as highly as I regard Toplady — and Ryle — is he overstating his praise of Toplady as a hymn-writer? 'Rock of Ages' most certainly is one of the finest English hymns, but most of Toplady's poetic efforts fall short of its richness and pathos. Nevertheless, there are several of his hymns that are very fine and — like Toplady himself — deserve to be better known and loved.

Polemics over poetry

Toplady's doctrinal zeal at times had a detrimental effect on his poetry. I wonder reading some of his poetry — poetry I have never sung or seen in church hymnals I have been familiar with — if he failed to keep the purpose of poetry before his mind as he wrote. The strength and sphere of poetry is more for adorning truth — what Toplady does so magnificently in 'Rock of Ages' — than declaring or propounding it. I am reminded of the self-criticism of Unitarian poet and literary critic James Russell Lowell (1819–1891), who wrote of his own poetic limitations:

> The top of the hill he will ne'er come nigh reaching
> Till he learns the distinction 'twixt singing and preaching.

In lines from his 'Hymn of Sovereign Grace', Toplady seems to suffer from the same limitation. True as his words are, one feels more the thunder of the polemicist than the passion of the penitent in the declarative lines:

> Thy Spirit does not offer life,
> But raises from the dead;
> And neither asks the sinner's leave,
> Nor needs the sinner's aid.

This is more a thesis/argument poem, a versified essay, than a hymn. If Ryle tended to overstate his praise of Toplady, hymnologist Erik Routley (1917–1982) unfairly disparages his poetic gift. 'Toplady could write', he said, 'that is to say, he could write prose, for he was no poet'. Measured by the above quatrain alone, Routley might be able to defend his statement.

In another stanza, Toplady seems again to be more the polemicist than the poet, yet he captures in a few succinct lines the truth that good works do not save us, nor do they keep us saved. Good works are the fruit of God's sovereign power first renewing the tree:

Thy power, before the fruit is good,
Must first renew the tree;
We rise, and work the works of God,
When wrought upon by thee.

This is good theology, but not great hymn poetry. Though it imbeds right theology in verse, it lacks the impassioned grace necessary to awaken the heart and imagination of the worshipper to the high praise of God. I suspect Toplady felt rather good about the salvo delivered from the metrical canon of these lines. I equally suspect that since he wrote these lines they have only rarely found their way into the singing of Christian worship. The tone and syntax lend themselves more to preaching than singing. The best hymns adorn the doctrinal truths of the gospel with passion, skill, and grateful adoration. And Toplady on a few occasions did just that.

Debtor to mercy alone

We can always count on Toplady to get the gospel right; that is without argument. In a hymn written in 1771, Toplady not only got the gospel right, but he achieved more of that passionate adorning quality so essential to a great hymn.

A debtor to mercy alone,
Of covenant mercy I sing;
Nor fear, with thy righteousness on,
My person and offering to bring.
The terrors of law and of God
With me can have nothing to do;
My Saviour's obedience and blood
Hide all my transgressions from view.

Toplady is not here the determined polemicist, parrying the thrust of his Arminian attackers. He is the trembling, awe-struck Christian, on his face in gratitude for the imputed righteousness of Jesus applied to his unworthy life.

> The work which his goodness began
> The arm of his strength will complete;
> His promise is Yea and Amen,
> And never was forfeited yet.
> Things future, nor things that are now,
> Not all things below nor above
> Can make him his purpose forego,
> Or sever my soul from his love.

Though not his finest lines of poetry, yet here Toplady turns the forgiven sinner away from himself and to the promises of the gospel, to the Heavenly Father who began a good work in redeemed sinners and, as promised, will perform it until the day of Jesus Christ (Philippians 1:6). For Toplady it is God's arm of strength that is the basis of Christian assurance, not our performance. God never reneges on his promises; hence the frailest Christian is assured because he is hidden in Christ. The saints in heaven may be more happy now than chronically-ill Toplady was when he penned these indelible lines, but they are not more secure than any Christian is in the present, hidden as we are in the cleft of Jesus' blood and righteousness.

> My name from the palms of his hands
> Eternity will not erase;
> Impressed on his heart it remains
> In marks of indelible grace.

Yea, I to the end shall endure,
As sure as the earnest is given.
More happy, but not more secure,
The glorified spirits in heaven.

There is an intimate, personal quality to these lines, and
though they portray Toplady's own heart and experience of
grace, they encompass a universal application that extends
to all worshipping Christians. What confidence does the
timorous Christian gain when taking Toplady's words on his
own lips! Do any more thrilling words of assurance exist in
the canon of Christian hymns?

More happy, but not more secure,
The glorified spirits in heaven.

'But not more secure.' And why not more secure? Toplady
understood that because of the imputed righteousness of
Christ, the Christian is righteous before God now. Though
we grow in grace, though we are being sanctified, 'the work
of God's free grace' in us, our righteous standing before God,
secured by the active obedience of Christ our righteousness,
makes our standing with God absolutely secure. Yes, we
certainly do look forward to glorification in heaven, but we
will not be more secure in heaven than we are right now
in Christ. Such is the soul-comforting theology Toplady
celebrates in this hymn.

Reformed University Fellowship campus pastor Kevin
Twit borrowed the name of his music ministry from
the fourth line of Toplady's final stanza, 'indelible grace.'
Kevin discovered the Toplady hymn while scouring C. H.
Spurgeon's *Our Own Hymnbook* for biblically rich lyrics,

accessible to university students at Belmont University, Nashville, Tennessee. When he discovered Toplady, he knew he had found what he was searching for. Indelible grace, for Toplady, is grace that no created thing can erase, grace that is impossible to remove or rub out, grace that is indelible, that remains for ever.

It sounds redundant: grace that really is grace. Can there be any other kind of grace? But because we proud sinners are constantly tampering with the gospel, redefining grace to include just a little bit of our obedience or our faithfulness, every generation is forced to employ adjectives and superlatives to get into our stubborn hides that salvation is entirely the free, unmerited gift of a stupendously merciful God.

How vast the benefits divine

In another hymn of Toplady that deserves to be sung more often by the church, he seemed to anticipate how theological revisionists would tamper with the gospel and the meaning of sanctification today. Did he have a premonition that there would be future generations within the church who would be suspicious that preaching free grace will lead to Antinomianism; men who are fearful that proclaiming the good news that Jesus truly paid it all would undermine morality and good works?

> How vast the benefits divine which we in Christ possess!
> Saved from the guilt of sin we are and called to holiness
> But not for works which we have done, or shall hereafter
>   do,
> Hath God decreed on sinful worms salvation to bestow.

The Father's saving purpose in Christ had nothing to do with our fitness before regeneration or our fitness after. Toplady did indeed understand that we have been chosen for holiness, but he never lost his grip on the fact that it is God who is at work in his elect to accomplish what he promises, both in justification and sanctification. Toplady understood that only when salvation is by grace alone, through faith alone, in Christ alone, would God receive all the glory alone.

> The glory, Lord, from first to last, is due to thee alone;
> Aught to ourselves we dare not take, or rob thee of thy
>   crown.
> Our glorious Surety undertook to satisfy for man,
> And grace was given us in him before the world began.

Certainly Toplady is on solid theological ground here, though perhaps not soaring on the highest plane of poetic imagery, the final line of the quatrain sounding the polemicist's cymbal more than the poet's clarion. Nevertheless, there are few hymns that achieve the same degree of soteriological clarity coupled with poetry as this hymn.

> This is thy will, that in thy love we ever should abide;
> And lo; we earth and hell defy to make thy counsel void.
> Not one of all the chosen race but shall to Heav'n attain,
> Partake on earth the purposed grace and then with Jesus
>   reign.

One need only read Wesley on free will and conditional justification to understand why Toplady felt compelled to conclude this hymn with soaring Pauline confidence.

Equally, one need only read Paul in Romans 8: 'There is therefore now no condemnation for those who are in Christ Jesus... For I am sure that neither death nor life, nor angels nor rulers, nor things present nor things to come, nor powers, nor height nor depth, nor anything else in all creation, will be able to separate us from the love of God in Christ Jesus our Lord' (ESV). Not earth nor hell. When he is for us, who can be against us? For Toplady, purposed grace meant that grace by its very definition is certain: it was purposed in God's eternal, merciful decree 'that in thy love we ever should abide'. Or as he expressed it so beautifully:

Grace, 'tis a charming sound,
Harmonious to the ear;
Heaven with the echo shall resound,
And all the earth shall hear.

11

A FRUITFUL LIFE

Like the Apostle Paul, Toplady was content with weakness (2 Corinthians 12:10). 'I cannot help observing,' he wrote on Monday 5 September 1768, 'that great humiliations are, often, the best preparations for ministerial usefulness.' 'The glory of young men is their strength' (Proverbs 20:29), and nothing confronts a young man's delusion of strength more than ill-health. Being sick all the time is humiliating. And yet Toplady, like Paul, gloried in his weakness, 'that the power of Christ may rest upon me' (2 Corinthians 12:9b).

The final stanza of another worthy but lesser-known hymn of Toplady's expresses his Pauline acknowledgment that 'when I am weak, then I am strong' (2 Corinthians 12:10b, ESV), that he needed the grace of divine strengthening in order daily to use his gifts for God's glory and to live each day of the short life he was given for God.

O let thy grace inspire
My soul with strength divine;
May all my powers to thee aspire,
And all my days be thine.

Fear of death

When Toplady told his physician that he was going to step into his pulpit one last time, the good doctor, certain it would kill him, begged him not to do it. Toplady would do it anyway, and, yes, it probably hastened his death. But he had for years been living and ministering as a 'dying man to dying men', and with daily reminders of his mortality and the frailty of his health. He recorded in his diary, after a day of pain and discomfort:

> *All day within. The former part of it I was considerably out of order: and experienced something of what it is to have a body without health, and a soul without comfort. But, while I was musing, the fire kindled, and the light of God's countenance shone within.*

This was so frequently Toplady's experience that it is not difficult to find such passages throughout his writings. And as a scholar and humble theologian, Toplady often turned to the sermons of great preachers, not only for instruction in good preaching, but for solace in times of suffering. Following immediately on his entry above, he wrote, 'I found a particular blessing in reading Mr. Mayo's sermon on our "Deliverance by Christ from the fear of Death" (Hebrews 2:15)'. He then observed:

> *Several things, in that choice discourse, struck me much... The apostle says, (1 Thessalonians 4:14) that Jesus died; but that the saints sleep in him: the reason why the phrase is varied, is because he sustained death with all its terrors, that so it might become a calm and quiet sleep to the saints.*

Imagine the comfort of these words to a sick man at the end of a long day of ministry. This was no theoretical exercise for chronically-ill Toplady. Imagine him sitting up, holding the book of sermons closer to the candlelight, hungrily soaking in Mr. Mayo's biblical instruction:

> *Satan desired to have Peter that he might sift him as wheat; and with what did he sift and shake him? Why, it was with the fear of death. Peter was afraid they would deal with him, as they were dealing with his master. It was his slavish fear of death, that made him deny Christ; but anon, he recovered himself, and got over his fear; how came this about? It was by means of faith. Christ had prayed for him that his faith should not fail.*

He then drew general conclusions from his observations:

> *It may be said of those who are fearful of death that they are of little faith. It is usual with God to give His people some clusters of the grapes of Canaan here in the wilderness; to give them some drops of that new wine, which they shall drink in the kingdom of their Father. This sets them a longing to have their fill thereof; even as the Gauls, when they had tasted the wines of Italy, were not satisfied to have those wines brought to them, but would go to possess the land where the vines grew.*

Notice the scholar-historian turning his knowledge of ancient history and wine to spiritual metaphor for the refreshment of his own soul in trouble.

No complaining

People who are sick, especially chronically sick, often talk, and complain, about their health to others. But Toplady did not spend time complaining in his writings, and only occasionally mentions his 'indispositions' of body. And always when he does he draws heavenly wisdom from his ill health.

After a day of particular weakness of body, he wrote, 'In the afternoon my indisposition was, in great measure, removed. Surely the shedding abroad of divine love in the heart, and a good hope through grace, frequently conduce as much to the health of the body as to the health of the soul. This is not the first time I have found it so.' And after riding home on horseback on 'a day most intense cold', Toplady observed,

> I have, through the blessing of God, been perfectly well through this whole day, both as to health, strength, and spirits; and gone through my church duties with the utmost ease, freedom and pleasure, yet I have experienced nothing of that comfort and spiritual joy, which I sometimes do.

Toplady's fellow hymn-writer, William Cowper, who suffered from depression, once observed that 'illness sanctified is better than health'. But it was in a hymn that Cowper memorably encapsulated what God can and often does in times of spiritual dryness:

> When comforts are declining,
> He grants the soul again
> A season of clear shining,
> To cheer it after rain.

Frail Toplady knew about dryness, especially when accompanied by physical weakness. After a day of ministry in which he felt little of Divine presence with him, he expresses deep longing for the reality, beauty, and sweetness of communion with the Holy Spirit. In sanctified soliloquy, he makes a case for the superiority of spiritual comforts when bodily health is at its weakest:

I myself am a witness, that spiritual comforts are sometimes highest, when bodily health, strength, and spirits, are at the lowest; and when bodily health, strength, and spirits are at the highest, spiritual comforts are sometimes at the lowest; nay, clear gone, and totally absent. Whence I conclude, that the sensible effusion of divine love in the soul, is superior to, independent of, and distinct from, bodily health, strength, and spirits.

Preparing to die

In February 1778, Toplady drew up his will. He had no heirs and he had few possessions to leave behind:

I most humbly commit my soul to Almighty God, whom I honour, and have long experienced to be my ever gracious and infinitely merciful Father. Nor have I the least doubt of my election, justification, and eternal happiness, through the riches of his everlasting and unchangeable kindness to me in Christ Jesus, his co-equal Son, my only, my assured, and my all-sufficient Saviour; washed in whose propitiatory blood, and clothed with whose imputed righteousness, I trust to stand perfect, sinless, and complete; and do verily believe that I most certainly shall stand, in the hour of death, and in the kingdom of heaven, and at the last judgment, and in the ultimate state of endless glory.

He proceeded next to render 'the deepest, the most solemn, and the most ardent thanks to the adorable Trinity in Unity, for their eternal, unmerited, irreversible, and inexhaustible love to me a sinner':

I bless God the Father for having written from everlasting my unworthy name in the book of life — even for appointing me to obtain salvation through Jesus Christ my Lord.

I adore God the Son for having vouchsafed to redeem me by his own most precious death, and for having obeyed the whole law for my justification.

I admire and revere the gracious benignity of God the Holy Ghost, who converted me to the saving knowledge of Christ more than twenty-two years ago, and whose enlightening, supporting, comforting, and sanctifying agency is, and (I doubt not) will be my strength and song in the hours of my earthly pilgrimage.

Toplady had little to leave behind him, but he knew and trusted without a doubt the indelible grace and all-sufficiency of the one who was rich but became poor so that Toplady through his poverty might become rich (2 Corinthians 8:9).

Dying in Jesus

Less than two months before Toplady's death, Wesley managed to circulate a report that Toplady, as he neared his end, had disavowed his Calvinism. It is speculated that Wesley thought Toplady too near his end to respond to the report. He miscalculated. On 14 June 1778, with his death imminent, Toplady stepped into the pulpit on Orange Street, London, one last time. His text was 2 Peter 1:13-14: 'Yea, I think it meet, as long as I am in this tabernacle, to stir you up by putting you in remembrance; knowing that shortly I must put off this my tabernacle, even as our Lord Jesus Christ hath shewed me.'

An eyewitness described Toplady's demeanour while delivering his final sermon:

> When speaking of the abundant peace he experienced, and the joy and consolation of the Holy Ghost, of which for months past he had been a partaker, together with the persuasion that in a few days he must resign his mortal part to corruption, as a prelude to seeing the King in His beauty, the effect produced was such as may, perhaps, be conceived, but certainly cannot at all be described.

The eyewitness continues his account of the disposition of Toplady as death approached:

> All his conversations, as he approached nearer and nearer to his decease, seemed more heavenly and happy. He frequently called himself the happiest man in the world. 'O!' (says he) 'how this soul of mine longs to be gone! Like a bird imprisoned in a cage, it longs to take its flight. O that I had wings like a dove, then would I flee away to the realms of bliss and be at rest forever!'

As heavenly-minded as this expression of longing for heaven is, and coming from a relatively young man, facing dying at only thirty-seven years old, it may seem to our ears an almost impossible attitude to sustain. Apparently it seemed so to one of those who was at his bedside:

> Being asked by a friend if he always enjoyed such manifestations, he answered, 'I cannot say there are no intermissions; for, if there were not, my consolations would be more than I could possibly bear; but when they abate they leave such an abiding sense of God's goodness and of the certainty of my being fixed upon the eternal Rock Christ Jesus, that my soul is still filled with peace and joy'.

A close friend gave this account of one of his last conversations with Toplady:

> A remarkable jealousy was apparent in his whole conduct as he drew near his end, for fear of receiving any part of that honour which is due to Christ alone. He desired to be nothing, and that Jesus might be all and in all. His feelings were so very tender upon this subject, that I once undesignedly put him almost in an agony by remarking the great loss which the Church of Christ would sustain by his death at this particular juncture. The utmost distress was immediately visible in his countenance, and he exclaimed, 'What! By my death? No, no! Jesus Christ is able, and will, by proper instruments defend his own truths. And with regard to what little I have been able to do in this way, not to me, not to me, but to his own name, and to that only, be the glory.'

Another friend, after speaking with Toplady about his last public words delivered at the Orange Street Chapel, recorded Toplady's 'practical and heartfelt experience' of the comfort the doctrines of grace brought to him when facing death:

> *My dear friend, these great and glorious truths, which the Lord in rich mercy has given me to believe, and which he has enabled me (though very feebly) to defend, are not, as those who oppose them say, dry doctrines or mere speculative points. No! being brought into practical and heartfelt experience, they are the very joy and support of my soul; and the consolations flowing from them carry me far above the things of time and sense. So far as I know my own heart, I have no desire but to be entirely passive, to live, to die, to be, to do, to suffer whatever is God's blessed will concerning me, being perfectly satisfied that as he ever has, so he ever will do that which is best concerning me, and that he deals out in number, weight and measure, whatever will conduce most to his own glory and to the good of his people.*

When he was asked about the rumours that had been spread that he had recanted his belief in the electing love of God for sinners, Toplady replied with feeling and more vigour than would be expected from a dying man: 'I recant my former principles! God forbid that I should be so vile an apostate!' After a pause, he added: 'And yet that apostate would I soon be, if I were left to myself'.

In another such account — there are many — Toplady's friend described his frame of mind as death neared. 'He appeared not merely placid and serene, but he evidently possessed the fullest assurance of the most triumphant faith.' The eyewitness described that as Toplady's body declined and his death loomed closer, his mind became 'more vigorous, lively, and rejoicing'. With each visit, as his health grew worse, 'he so earnestly longed to be dissolved and to be with Christ. His soul seemed to be constantly panting heavenward, and his desire increased the nearer his dissolution approached.'

After asking a friend to take his pulse, Toplady wanted to know what his friend thought. 'I told him that his heart and arteries evidently beat almost every day weaker and weaker.' Toplady's immediate reply, with smiling face was, 'Why, that is a good sign that my death is fast approaching; and, blessed be God, I can add that my heart beats every day stronger and stronger for glory.' The eyewitness accounts continue:

A few days before his dissolution I found him sitting up in his arm-chair, but scarcely able to move or speak. I addressed him very softly, and asked if his consolations continued to abound as they had hitherto done. He quickly replied, 'O my dear sir, it is impossible to describe how good God is to me. Since I have been sitting in this chair this afternoon I have enjoyed such a season, such sweet communion with God, and such delightful manifestation of his presence with, and love to my soul, that it is impossible for words or any language to express them. I have had peace and joy unutterable, and I fear not but that God's consolation and support will continue.' But he immediately recollected himself, and added, 'What have I said? God may, to be sure, as a sovereign, hide his face and smiles from me; however,

I believe he will not; and if he should, yet will I trust him. I know I am safe and secure, for his love and his covenant are everlasting!'

When death was imminent, Toplady motioned his friends and servants to his bedside. His final words were written down by those who heard them. After their expressions of regret at losing him but willingness for him to depart and be with Christ, he said, 'Oh, what a blessing it is that you are made willing to give me up into the hands of my dear Redeemer, and to part with me! It will not be long before God takes me; for no mortal man can live, after the glories which God has manifested to my soul.'

Augustus Montague Toplady died on Tuesday 11 August 1778. He was thirty-seven years old. He was buried where he had first heard George Whitefield preach, at Tottenham Court Chapel, below the gallery, across from the pulpit. Thousands from all over London came to pay their respects to the young pastor and hymn-writer. Though Toplady had expressly forbidden anyone to give honour to him at his funeral, there were words expressing gratitude to God for giving to the church such a one as Toplady. His earthly resting place at Tottenham Court Chapel was bombed into oblivion during World War II.

Vilifying ashes

As controversy had been so much a part of Toplady's life, so it followed him even after his death. The funeral and burial barely concluded when Wesley for some reason felt the need to circulate a public declaration about his version of Toplady's final days and words. In direct contradiction to the host of eyewitnesses who were at Toplady's side when he died, Wesley declared that Toplady 'died in black despair, uttering the most horrible blasphemies, and that none of his friends were permitted to see him'.

Two friends of Toplady's, Sir Richard Hill (1732–1808) and the Rev. J. Gawkrodger (d.1798), a Calvinistic Baptist minister, could not remain silent at this slander and falsehood. They wrote to Wesley and accused him 'of vilifying the ashes and traducing the memory of the late Mr. Augustus Toplady', reaffirming that 'many respectable witnesses could testify that Mr. Toplady departed this life in the full triumph of faith'. Others joined in defence of Toplady, one a Nonconformist pastor who wrote a pamphlet confronting Wesley for persecuting Toplady in his lifetime and for 'sprinkl[ing] his deathbed with abominable falsehood'. He concluded:

> Wretched must that cause be, which has need to be supported by such unmanly shifts, and seek for shelter under such disingenuous subterfuges. O! Mr. Wesley, answer for this conduct at the bar of the Supreme Judge yourself and you shall not be judged. Dare you also to persuade your followers that Mr. Toplady actually died in despair! Fie upon sanctified slander! Fie! Fie!

A sweet departure

An obscure hymn of Toplady gives us a still more intimate and sanctified window into his posture toward his failing health and early death. The heading before Hymn XXIV reads, 'Written in Illness. Psalm 104: 34. "My meditation of him shall be sweet"':

> When languor and disease invade
> This trembling house of clay,
> 'Tis sweet to look beyond the cage,
> And long to fly away.

The next seven stanzas begin with the word 'Sweet', and in the eighth stanza he considers his own dying and deathbed.

> Sweet to rejoice in lively hope,
> That, when my change shall come,
> Angels will hover round my bed,
> And waft my spirit home.

Toplady could not have known for certain that he was to have so few years in this life, yet his coughing had persisted, as had the painful in-drawing of breath, caused by his 'insidious disease of the chest'. These constant reminders of his mortality had served to sober him and make him live each day as if it may be his last, and at the same time, to live with a joyful expectancy of heaven.

Toplady's patience in affliction and his anticipation of heaven while serving here below run counter to our modern sensibilities that shun the thought of death. In this, Toplady serves as a model for us. He was not deceived about death and dying, and he did not want his congregation to be so either.

The final stanza of Augustus Montague Toplady's best-loved hymn perfectly encapsulates the Christian's attitude toward death. Countless Christians have felt that thrill of gospel assurance at Christ's promise of eternal life expressed so enduringly by Toplady:

> While I draw this fleeting breath,
> When my eyelids close in death.
> When I soar to worlds unknown,
> See thee on thy judgment throne.
> Rock of Ages, cleft for me,
> Let me hide myself in thee!

Toplady was a scholar and theologian, but such have the ear of only the educated few. He was a fine preacher, but preachers primarily speak to a single generation. It was the Archbishop husband of a hymn-writer who got it right: 'The hymn-writer speaks an imperishable language.'

FURTHER READING

For readers interested in delving more closely into the life of Augustus Toplady, I recommend John Charles Ryle's fair and appreciative short biography published by The Banner of Truth Trust in *Christian Leaders of the 18th Century*. For those interested in reading more of Toplady's lesser-known hymns, his *Hymns and Sacred Poems* and his *Psalms and Hymns for Public and Private Worship*, though both out of print, are available on-line. Along with many of his hymns, in the volume *Diary and Selection of Hymns of Augustus Toplady* one will find many insights into his life and ministry in his honest and detailed diary entries. For more in-depth investigation of his theological writings, *A Caveat Against Unsound Doctrines*, *Historic Proof of the Doctrinal Calvinism of the Church of England*, and *The Works of Augustus M. Toplady*, though not in print, may be found in archives on the internet.